Stock Market Advanced Trading: 3 Hour Crash Course

The ultimate cashflow guide for diversified investing

Edward Day

from various sources. Please consult a licensed professional before attempting any techniques outlined in this book.

By reading this document, the reader agrees that under no circumstances is the author responsible for any losses, direct or indirect, that are incurred as a result of the use of the information contained within this document, including, but not limited to, errors, omissions, or inaccuracies.

Table of Contents

"Being rich isn't a privilege. Being rich is a right. If you create massive value for others, you have the right to be as rich as you want."
— *Steve Siebold*

Introduction

Have you ever watched *The Wolf of Wall Street* and envied Jordan Belfort's lifestyle just a little? The fast cars, the ginormous yachts, the private jets, and the exotic locations? I think it's only human for the green-eyed jealousy monster to make its appearance when one is confronted with that amount of wealth. In fact, envy is an evolutionary response that humans have developed in order to make sure that we're always striving to be better and to have more — it's nothing you have to feel guilty about. Envy is so ingrained into our response systems that most children start complaining about their siblings supposedly getting more soda, a larger slice of pizza, or a bigger scoop of ice cream than they did as soon as they learn to talk. There are basically only two ways to deal with envy: you either make peace with it and try to push the feeling to the back of your mind, or you see it as a challenge to acquire that which caused you to become envious in the first place. Successful stock traders see it as the latter.

You have a seven percent chance of becoming a millionaire in your lifetime, and a 0.00018% chance of becoming a billionaire. Credit Suisse estimates that there are about 50 million millionaires in the world, and just under half of them can be found right here in the

United States of America. Other than the USA, five other countries also yield an almost abnormal amount of millionaires: China, Japan, France, Germany, and the United Kingdom. It might feel like the odds are stacked against you, but if I offered you a candy bar and said that you'd have a 7% risk of dying if you were to eat it, you wouldn't eat it — seven percent is a lot more than it sounds.

W.C. Fields (William Claude Dukenfield) once said that the only difference between a poor man and a rich man was money, and as idiotic as the statement may sound — it's true. Stock market billionaires also wake up in the morning with dragon breath and scruffy hair, they also get acne, and suffer from the sniffles every now and then, they're human too. The fact that they're human, just like you, and that you're not all that different means that everything that they have achieved is within your reach as well. There's nothing 'special' about them that makes them rich, they got that way (and stayed that way) through hard work, dedication, clever investing, and by conscientiously investing every spare penny.

However, science has found that millionaires share five common personality traits: extroversion, narcissism, conscientiousness, emotional stability, and they're less prone to neuroticism. This means that your average millionaire investor is laid back, enjoys spending time with friends and family, believes that he or she is destined for greater things, is careful with his or her money and investments, and isn't prone to bouts of negativity or anxiousness. The culmination of these traits in an individual makes them less likely to panic and sell their stocks when the stock market takes a downturn or to buy up shares because of hype caused by the media or their fellow investors, while ensuring that he or she is forever chasing higher returns on the stock market.

A study conducted by Thomas Corley also found that two-thirds of millionaires spent less than an hour a day watching television or browsing the internet. What do millionaires do with all of their extra time? Well, it seems that they spend it on work. The same study found that approximately 86% of millionaires work more than 50 hours a week (that's about an hour and 15 minutes of extra work a day when compared to your average American who only works 44 hours per week on average). Millionaires don't just look after their bank accounts' well being either, three-quarters of them exercise four or more times a week, making your average millionaire a lot healthier than your average Joe. Luckily these traits aren't reserved for the rich and famous, you can actively work on embodying more of them in your personal and professional life. 'Mirroring' other professional investors is a well-recognized and respected technique, but you can take it further than simply matching their stock picks by also matching their mannerisms and habits.

Mark Zuckerberg, the Facebook-mogul, was only 23 when he made his first billion dollars. Stories like Mark's can make older investors feel like they've missed their window of opportunity, but this simply is not true. Fidelity's *Millionaire Outlook Survey* found that most investors took 32 years' in order to build up their portfolios to the point that they were worth $1 million (in fact, four-fifths of millionaires only make their first million after the age of 50). You don't need to be a spring chicken in order to start making your way to being able to afford a lifestyle like Jordan Belfort's (before he was sent to prison).

Many people argue that being a millionaire is a privilege reserved for those who were already born into wealth, but this is a fallacy too (and a very commonly propagated one at that). Research conducted in 2016 found that approximately four-fifths of all millionaires were raised in poor or lower middle-class households, which means that only 22% of them were born into wealthy families. These 'poor' millionaires all have one thing in common — they were raised by strict parents who expected either academic or financial success from their children.

Of course, millionaires don't become millionaires just by wishing for it (although Thomas Corley did find that just a bit more than half of all millionaires were obsessed with becoming millionaires long before actually becoming one), it takes some hard work, a dash of luck, and a well planned investment strategy too.

A study conducted by the Spectrem Group found that over 40% of all millionaires credit their wealth to a well thought out investment strategy. These investment strategies often involve an awful lot of savings. The Harris Group's *Survey of Affluence and Wealth* found that investors who saved and reinvested about a quarter of their income were the most likely to eventually become millionaires. These investors don't stop being smart with their money once their millionaires either, as surveys have found that four-fifths of all active millionaires spend less than $100,000 on vacations annually and three-quarters of them don't gamble, ever. By keeping their expenses low, millionaires are able to keep reinvesting back in the stock market, exponentially increasing the value of their portfolios with every reinvestment.

While being a bit more sociable and frugal is definitely a start, you need to do more if you're hoping to become a millionaire. Luckily the stock market is the place to be if you're hoping to be the next Bill Ackman. The United States of America's Internal Revenue Service (IRS) found in their report, *The 400 Individual Tax Returns Reporting the Largest Adjusted Gross Incomes*, that out of the 400 highest earning individuals in the United States, about 260 made their wealth off of capital gains from selling stocks. There's more than enough wealth going around on the stock market, you just need to know how to tap into it — fortunately for you, that's exactly what this book is going to teach you how to do.

An Introduction to 'Me' and My Trading History

Satchel Paige, the world-renowned baseball player, said that women and money were similar in the sense that you'd do absolutely anything to acquire either. I didn't get involved in forex trading in order to attract women though, I got into it to make enough money to give my wife and daughters the kind of life that they deserve. I'm sure that that's why many of you are interested in increasing your net worth through the stock market too — in order to finance your families' dream lifestyles. Many of the world's most famous millionaires are family-people whose immediate relations mean the world to them. A study titled *Insights on Wealth and Worth* showed that nearly four-fifths of all millionaires are married, with more than 60% of them having never had a divorce. Successful investors need something to hold on to that encourages them to keep working towards their financial goals, for many people this inspiration takes the form of a spouse or children (if not both). Your motivation might be something entirely different though: it might be to someday own a small island off of the coast of Brazil, or to purchase a personalized helicopter, or perhaps you'd just like to be able to rent a home with a bigger garden for your dog.

I've always been a little in love with money and finance. I went off to study a bachelor's degree in finance straight out of high school, which I followed up by finishing a Master's degree in accounting. I walked straight out of university and into the waiting arms of an accounting firm. I worked as a chartered accountant for a few years, and although I enjoyed it, I felt that something was missing from my life. I carried this desire for 'something better' with me for what felt like eons, until the fateful day on which one of my clients invited me to a forex seminar. I was skeptical at first, but eventually agreed to go. I've always believed that fate works in mysterious ways, and I like to think that I was destined to end up accompanying my client to this seminar because it is what got me hooked on stock trading. It had such a profound effect on me that I decided to go back to university and complete a bachelor's degree in economics (as well as a myriad of forex trading courses). I devoured all of the information on stocks and stock trading that I could find, and soon found myself being invited to give talks at seminars on forex trading (just like the one that sparked my love for investing in foreign exchanges).

I'm not the only successful stock trader that carved my way to the top through education, a study conducted by the Spectrem Group found that approximately 84% of all millionaires are college educated and that a further 88% of them spent at least half an hour each day reading educational books in order to improve their understanding of economics and finance. Of course, you don't need a fancy degree in order to make millions, millionaires like Zhou Qunfei (who founded Lens Technology), Amancio Ortega (who started Zara), Francois Pinault (who pioneered the company called Kering), and Richard Branson (who famously founded Virgin) all became a part of the top 0.6% without even a high school diploma to their names. If you're willing to keep learning and expanding your knowledge of the stock market, you don't need a piece of paper to validate what you already know.

I'm not special just because I've 'made it big' on the stock market. In fact, we probably have a lot in common. I'm just your average American family guy who enjoys fishing on the weekends and taking my two dogs for walks. If an average guy like myself can do it, so can you. Fortunately for you, I've taken a liking to taking students under my wing — over the next six chapters I'm going to share all of the secrets that helped me to go from 'ordinary' to 'extraordinary' with you.

I'm Not The Only One Who Has Gotten Rich By Trading Stocks

I'm just a small fry compared to the big guys like Warren Buffett and George Soros, but I'm one of many normal Americans that have made a pretty penny by investing in the stock market.

George Soros is arguably the most inspirational successful stock trader of all time. He was born a Jew in the 1930s in Budapest, which means that his childhood was defined by the murder of 500,000 of his own people during the German Occupation of Hungary in 1944. George and his family only managed to survive because they craftily made falsified identity documents for themselves (and saved countless other Jewish families by helping them to do the same). The end of World War Two didn't see the end of George's strife. The rise of communism directly after the fall of the Nazis drove George to seek refuge in England where he worked as a railway porter in order to finance his studies through the London School of Economics. Shortly after graduating, George was offered a position at Singer and Friedlander, which is when his star really started to shine. George soon came to be known as the 'King of Forex' and is currently worth $8.3 billion (which is about four times as much as President Donald Trump is worth). George would be worth a lot more if he wasn't such a philanthropist — to date he has donated about $32 billion of his personal money to charity. The most important lesson which one can learn from George's story is that coming from a place of adversity doesn't determine the kind of life you're capable of living. The moral of the story is that hard work and determination is the solution to nearly any problem.

Warren Buffett (the current chief executive officer of Berkshire Hathaway) was born in Omaha in the 1930s, around the same time that George Soros was born. At age seven little Warren borrowed a book titled *One Thousand Ways to Make $1,000* from his local library, and he never looked back. His childhood attempts at making a million (or a thousand) dollars involved selling soda and chewing gum, and delivering magazines door-to-door on a kind of "paper route." At 11, Warren made his first investment in the stock market by purchasing three shares in Cities Service. His high school attempts at turning over a profit were a lot more successful. In his sophomore year, Warren and a friend purchased a pinball machine and got permission to put it in a local hair salon for clients' waiting children to play with. The venture was such a resounding success that Warren was able to sell it for $1,200 within a couple of months. He used this sum to purchase a 40-acre farm which he leased out to a neighboring farmer. Warren had big dreams long before most of us dreamed of anything other than being cowboys or princesses, so it's no surprise that he had amassed the equivalent of $105,000 in savings by the time he finished college (which his father had forced him to attend against his wishes). Warren has spent the rest of his life doing very much the same thing he did in high school: purchasing promising commodities, profiting off of their dividends, and then selling them once their price has increased beyond a certain point. At the moment Warren is worth about $76 billion and he's the fourth richest person in the world. Warren's life story is a testament to the fact that if you're willing to keep investing, you'll almost always see a profit. Warren might have started making money while most of us were still hunting fireflies, but it's never too late to adopt some of his habits, and to mimic some of his profits.

Peter Lynch's father died when he was only 10 years old, leaving his mother behind as the family's sole breadwinner. Times were tough in the Lynch household, and little Peter was forced to work as a caddy to help his mom make ends meet. By the time he got to high school, he had managed to save up a decent sum of money from lugging around golf bags and decided to invest it in Flying Tiger Airlines at $8 a share. Within a couple of months, Flying Tiger Airlines's shares increased in value by 1000% and Peter made his first decent profit on the stock market. Working as a caddy would prove advantageous to Peter in more than just one way too. Shortly after leaving high school, he was offered a job at Fidelity Investments by its president, George Sullivan, who had often made use of Peter's services as a caddy at Brae Burn Country Club. Today Peter has a net worth of about $450 million, and he's still actively investing in the stock market at the age of 76.

Bruce Kovner was born in New York in the 1940s, and although he had a good upbringing, his early adulthood was marred by his mother's suicide in 1965. Ten years later Bruce would find himself working as a cab driver. It was during this period in his life that he started considering investing in the stock market. He started off by saving some of the tips he received while on the job, and eventually (with the additional assistance of a loan) managed to invest $3,000 in soybean futures contracts. Bruce watched the value of his first investment skyrocket to $40,000, but naively waited too long to sell and only managed to offload his investment at $23,000 (nevertheless, the $20,000 worth of profit was more than enough to encourage him to keep investing in the stock market). Bruce is currently worth just over $5 billion at the age of 75.

There are thousands of people currently making a living off of stock trading, some of them make it big and earn billions. You'll never know if you could be one of them unless you take a leap of faith and go all in. Who would want to settle for a mediocre nine-to-five life when you could aim for the stars and spend next summer on a yacht in the Caribbean?

Don't Let a Bearish Stock Market Put You Off, Now Is A Better Time Than Ever to Invest

The S&P 500 Index, the Nasdaq Composite Index, and the Dow Jones Industrial Average Index have all experienced downward trajectories of more than 20% in the wake of one of the most prolific economic crises (caused by the outbreak of Covid-19) of our generation. The stock market has been wobbly and unpredictable lately at best, which has left many investors too scared to spend any money on shares and has encouraged just as many to dump shares whose prices have been negatively affected by the crisis. A bear market, like the one caused by Covid-19, causes share prices to dramatically decrease, but that doesn't mean that it's a bad time to take your investment strategy to the next level. In fact, it offers smart investors a myriad of money-making opportunities.

One of the ways to profit from a bear market is to invest in an index fund just before the market becomes bearish or during its bearish phase. Index funds' values might plummet to nearly zero during a recession, but the stocks which they'll rake up for next to nothing during this time period will cause their dividends and pay-outs to increase nearly tenfold when the market starts recovering. It's easy to invest in index funds through your 401(k) or individual retirement account (IRA), if you have either. If you have neither, you can still invest in an index fund by approaching a stock brokerage firm. Some of the best, most consistent, index funds to invest in are The Schwab S&P 500 Fund (SWPPX), The Vanguard 5oo Index Fund (VFIAX), The Fidelity 500 Index Fund (FXAIX), and the T. Rowe Price Equity Index Fund (PREIX). The Vanguard 5oo Index Fund requires a minimum investment of $3,000, while The T. Rowe Price Equity Index Fund requires a minimum investment of $2,500 — the remaining index funds have no required minimum investment which means that you could technically invest in them with nothing but $100 to your name.

Another way to profit off of the flailing economy is to invest in long- and short term puts during a stock's downward trajectory. A 'put' is a right that you buy from a stockbroker to sell 100 specific shares at a predetermined price to him during a specified period of time. This concept might make a little more sense in the form of an example. Imagine that you receive a tip off that a stock that is currently selling for $100 per share is about to drastically decrease in value because of some management scandal. With this knowledge you could approach a stockbroker and purchase a 'put' for $100 on those stocks, binding the stockbroker to buying them from you for $95 per share over the next two months should you choose to call-up the put during that time period. Let's say the stock's price falls to $10 per share over the first month, if you were to put the 'put' you'd purchased earlier in action the stockbroker would be obliged to buy the agreed-to 100 shares for a total of $9,500. If you hadn't put the 'put' in place, you would have only been able to sell those 100 shares for $1,000 (which means you would have lost a potential $8,500 on the trade). A put is only useful if you're sure that the stock's price is going to continue to decline and if the stock in question isn't considered to be a long term investment, this means that it's not the perfect recession-strategy for everyone.

The recession created by the Coronavirus offers keen investors the rare opportunity to buy high value and growth stocks for a fraction of their usual prices. No bear market has lasted longer than 428 days, which means that stock prices are bound to start recovering in about a year's time at the latest. This means that you could buy stock in a blue chip company like Apple for next to nothing during a recession, only to sell it again once the market recovers and it regains its original value.

There are a number of ways you could go about buying profitable stocks during a recession, though you need to be mindful that your money is likely to be tied up in any stock market investments which you make during a bear market for at least twelve months (after which the stock market should start improving). Blue chip stocks will always be a good investment, even during uncertain times. Consequently, investors should consider buying shares belonging to companies with large market capitalizations that have significantly decreased in price due to the pressures of a recession — once they've acquired these shares they can either sell them for a profit once the market recovers, or they can hold onto them and profit off of their dividends. Blue chip stocks are generally very generous with their dividend payments. Some of the best blue chip stocks which you can currently invest in belong to Abbott Laboratories (that is working towards supplying a molecular diagnostic test for the Coronavirus), Bristol Myers Squibb (that manufactures many types of chronic medication which people will continue to need regardless of what the current epidemic does to the economy), and JPMorgan Chase (a respected bank whose stock price has fallen by more than 40% since the Corona crisis started).

Another option is to invest in stocks belonging to companies that are set to profit off of the current pandemic, like those belonging to pharmaceutical companies that are working on producing a Coronavirus vaccine or treatment, or who are involved in supplying or manufacturing ventilators, medical masks, or gloves.

The race is on to see which company will be able to cure the Coronavirus, and Gilead Sciences is determined to cross the finish line first. A drug which Gilead Sciences originally developed to treat the Ebola virus in central Africa has been shown to be an effective treatment for the Coronavirus as well, and although further tests are needed before its efficacy can be scientifically confirmed, buying in now might see you laughing all the way to the bank if Gildead's miracle drug is found to cure Covid-19. The outbreak of the Coronavirus has also re-emphasized the importance of proper hygiene, which means that disinfectant companies are having their moment in the sun. Market analysts agree that buying into companies like Clorox now could see investors pocketing hefty dividends a couple of months down the line. Social distancing has also changed the way that the public interacts with medical professionals and Teladoc, a company that facilitates virtual doctors' appointments, is cashing in on this fact — which makes it a fantastic choice for the more daring investor.

Medical companies aren't the only ones profiting off of the current epidemic and related lockdowns. As more and more businesses are forced to learn how to operate remotely, more and more of them are making use of virtual workspaces like those offered by Zoom or Slack. This tendency has naturally translated into both Slack and Zoom's stock prices soaring. Investors who are willing to hedge some money on the fact that many businesses and professionals will continue offering "work-from-home" options to their employees after the crisis has passed may want to invest in either of the aforementioned companies, as if this is the case their value will continue to skyrocket over the next couple of months. Entertainment companies' stocks will also continue to increase in value for as long as the virus remains at the forefront of everyone's minds, which means that smart investors have already started stockpiling shares in Netflix, Electronic Arts, and Activision Blizzard.

Recessions are scary times for investors, but the most beautiful diamonds are often formed under the most extreme pressure. The current bear market offers clever investors a multitude of ways to strike gold, you just need to be brave enough to start digging.

Chapter 1:

A Brief Review of

Everything Stocks

Nobody likes admitting that they don't know enough about a certain subject, but a lack of knowledge in the stock market and how it operates can prove fatal to the financial goals of aspiring traders. Luckily this chapter spares you the possible embarrassment of having to ask someone for clarification on a stock market term, strategy, or point of reference by compressing everything you need to know into a couple of pages.

We can't discuss advanced stock market trading strategies unless you understand what the stock market is, what stocks are, and the importance of both. If you read the first book in this series, titled "*Stock Market 101*," you're probably already familiar with most of the concepts discussed below. However, the following discussions will be useful to you if you didn't read the first installment or if you simply feel that you need a refresher course on the basics of stock trading.

Stock Trading Terms Every Stock Trader Needs to Know

Stock traders have a language all their own just like doctors and lawyers do, and just as is the case with medical lingo or legalese, beginners need to put some effort into learning it in order to be able to master it. There are thousands (if not hundreds of thousands) of words, phrases, and terms that have specifically been coined by stockbrokers or traders in order to refer to elements of stock trading or the stock market, and although memorizing them all can be a daunting task, you can't be truly 'stock market literate' without them.

Some of the most important stock trading terms that all investors need to know are:

Acid test ratio: This is a test that investors use in order to determine whether a company's cash flow is healthy enough to sustain its future growth. It is measured by taking a company's short term assets and dividing them by its short term liabilities. Companies with acid test ratios of 1:1 are generally safe to invest in, however, companies with acid test ratios of 1:2 or less should be approached with caution. This test is also called a "quick ratio."

After-hours trading: Buying or selling stocks after the stock exchange's daily close. After-hours trading allows investors to adjust their portfolios as news breaks throughout the day (which means that it affords them the opportunity to react in a timely manner and avoid any possible resulting losses).

Aggressive growth funds: These are mutual funds that invest in high-risk, high-reward stocks.

Alpha: This is a measurement of a stock's performance when compared to one of the major stock market indices. Companies with a positive alpha value are growing faster than the stock market is, while companies with a negative alpha value are underperforming when compared to the rest of the companies on that particular stock exchange.

American depositary receipts (ADR): These are 'shares' in a foreign company that are issued by an American bank for the purpose of being exchanged and traded on an American stock exchange. Purchasing international stocks through ADRs is easier than accessing foreign stock exchanges in order to purchase them.

American-style option: This is an option that allows you to execute it at any time during the period which was specified in its agreement, up to and including the final day which it is valid for.

Appreciation funds: These are funds that invest in stocks that their fund managers believe are likely to significantly increase in value over time, offering their investors the chance to profit through capital appreciation.

Asian option: This is an option in which a stockbroker agrees to buy stocks from you at a price that is equal to their average price over a predetermined period of time.

Balanced funds: These are mutual funds that invest in a variety of bonds and stocks in order to offer their investors a diversified portfolio.

Bear market (or a bearish market): This is when the stock market experiences a sustained period of downward trajectory, leading to an average decline in stock prices and trader activity.

Beta: A stock's beta value tells investors how volatile it is. It is calculated by comparing the stock's price fluctuations over a three year period to that of the S&P 500. The higher a stock's beta value is, the riskier investing in it is.

Binary option (or binary trading): This is a type of investment that centers around a wager that the trader makes on whether a stock's price will increase or decrease. The trader only receives a payout if his or her prediction of the stock price's movement is correct, otherwise, he or she loses their entire investment and doesn't make a penny.

Bond funds: These are low-risk mutual funds that invest in preferred stocks and bonds, although the majority of their portfolios generally consist of bonds (hence their name).

Bull market: This is when the stock market experiences a sustained period of upward trajectory. It is characterized by increasing stock prices and an increase in trader activity.

Capital gain: This is calculated by subtracting the price which you purchased a stock for from the price which you sold it for.

Capital growth: The amount by which a stock's price has increased over a specified period of time.

Capital loss: The amount by which a stock's price has decreased over a specified period of time.

Cyclical stocks: These are stocks whose prices fluctuate in predictable 'cycles.' For example, stocks in a company that produces and sells ice cream will sell for more in the summer when the company is at its most profitable than it will in winter.

Currency futures contracts: These are agreements to purchase a predetermined currency for a specific sum on an agreed-to date (which means they're a little bit like options).

Decile rank: This is a measurement used to quantify a mutual fund's productivity by comparing its output to that of other similar mutual funds. The lower a mutual fund's decile rank is, the better it has performed. You should thus think twice about investing in mutual funds with high decile rankings.

Defensive stocks: This is a name given to shares that do not lose their value when the stock market goes through a bearish phase. Utilities (like water suppliers and electrical companies), consumer staples (like food or tobacco manufacturers), and stocks belonging to the healthcare sector are examples of defensive stocks.

Equity income funds: These are mutual funds that invest in blue chip stocks that regularly pay out hefty dividends to their investors.

European-style option: This is a type of option which can only be executed on the final day of the agreed-to period. In other words, if you had the option to buy 100 shares at $22 each for a two week period, you'd only be able to buy them at the end of that two week period.

Exchange-traded funds: These are funds that, like index funds, craft their portfolios to mimic the companies featured on major stock market indices. Unlike index funds, share in exchange traded funds are bought and sold on the stock market just like ordinary stocks.

Growth and income funds: These are exchange-traded or mutual funds that invest in a mixture of value and growth stock (which means that they offer their investors the chance to profit both through regular dividend payouts and through the stocks' capital appreciation).

Hedging: This is a strategy that investors use to minimize their possible losses should a stock that they've invested in suddenly devalue. There are numerous ways to hedge an investment, but the easiest is to buy a put-option on the stocks concerned. A put-option gives you the right to sell these stocks at a predetermined price for a specified period of time, which means that having one in place can allow you to recover your full investment even if a stock's price does suddenly plummet.

Hedge funds: These are private investment funds reserved for invited investors. Invitations to hedge funds are usually only issued to accomplished professional stock traders and incredibly wealthy investors. They operate in much the same way as mutual funds (described below) do in the sense that they pool investors' money to invest in a variety of different stocks and bonds. Hedge funds also often make use of borrowed capital in order to make these investments.

Income funds: These are exchange-traded or mutual funds that invest solely in stocks that offer their investors regular dividend payouts. They are not concerned with the capital appreciation of the stocks held within their portfolios.

Index funds: These are mutual funds that form their portfolios in order to mimic certain stock market indices. For example, the Schwab S&P 500 Index Fund invests in stocks belonging to the 500 companies that are listed on the S&P 500.

Indicated dividend: This is an estimation (calculated using a stock's most current dividend payout rate) of the value of dividends a certain stock will offer its investors in the following year.

International funds: There are mutual funds whose portfolios consist of stocks belonging to foreign companies.

Load funds: These are mutual funds that charge their investors commission fees in exchange for selecting the stocks held within the fund.

Long position: This is when an investor buys stocks that are expected to increase in value that he or she is planning to hold on to for a while.

Margin account: This is a type of stock trading account that some stock brokerage firms offer their investors. It allows investors to purchase commodities like shares and bonds on credit.

Municipal bond funds: These are funds that allow traders to invest in bonds that have been issued by the government.

Mutual funds: This is an investment tool that allows traders to invest in a diverse portfolio of stocks by investing in a single fund that buys and sells stocks on behalf of all of its investors. Investors' money is 'pooled' together in order to make these trades.

No-load funds: These are mutual funds that do not charge investors commission fees.

No-transaction-fee (NTF) funds: These are mutual funds that do not charge investors any transaction fees.

Option: Options are contracts that investors can buy which give them the right to buy an agreed-to number of stocks for a specific price within a predetermined period of time. Options are often used to 'hedge' (defined above) investments.

Option-income funds: These are mutual funds that generate profit for their investors by strategically buying and selling options.

Over-the-counter markets (OTC): These markets are not like traditional stock exchanges in the sense that buyers buy stocks directly from the seller. The market does not play a role in facilitating the exchange. Cheaper, high risk stocks are generally traded on OTC markets.

Penny stocks: These are higher risk stocks that usually trade through over-the-counter markets. They normally sell for less than $5 per share.

Program trading: Program trading involves using specially coded software to buy and sell stocks through different major stock exchanges in order to profit off of their price differences. For example, program trading may allow you to buy a share in Apple for $250 through the NYSE, and sell it within seconds for $249.90 on the Nasdaq. Traders who trade a large enough volume of stocks through program trading are generally able to make considerable profits.

Puts: A 'put' is the opposite of an option. It's a contract that can be purchased from a broker or brokerage firm which gives investors the right to sell a select number of shares for a specific price within a predetermined period of time to the issuing broker or brokerage firm.

Redemption: When you withdraw an amount of money from a mutual fund that you've invested in, it is called a 'redemption.'

Redemption fee: This is an amount of money you may be liable for paying if you withdraw a sum of money from a mutual fund that you've invested in before the period of time which was agreed to in the initial contract has passed (this period of time is normally anything from two to three months from the date of an investor's first investment in the fund).

Relative strength: This value, which is derived by comparing a stock's growth to that of one of the major indices, is used to analyze whether a certain stock would be a good investment or not. Stocks with a relative strength value of one or more are usually good investments, whereas stocks with a relative strength value of less than one are generally bad investments.

Rights offering: This is when investors who own shares in a specific company are approached by that company and offered further shares from an upcoming secondary offering at a reduced price.

Sector funds: These are mutual funds that exclusively invest in stocks belonging to the same sector. Some sector funds only invest in stocks belonging to medical companies, while others only invest in stocks belonging to technology or mining companies.

Shares repurchase programs: This is when a company offers to buy back some of its stocks which are owned by the general public. Companies usually offer these programs when they're hoping to decrease the dilution of ownership caused by an over-supply of their shares. Share prices generally significantly increase when their holding company starts running a repurchase program.

Short position: This is a trading strategy that involves selling stocks that you own just before their prices decrease, with the intention of buying them back on the devaluation that you've predicted has occurred.

Short selling: This is a trading strategy that involves borrowing stocks that you believe will soon start to decrease in price for a predetermined period of time from a fellow trader, broker, or brokerage firm. Traders making use of this strategy sell the borrowed stocks before their prices start declining, and then buy them back once they've devalued a sufficient amount. The borrowing trader then returns the stocks to the trader, broker, or brokerage firm that he or she had borrowed them from, and keeps the profit. An example of short selling would be if you borrowed 100 stocks worth $5 each from a friend until the end of the month, sold them for $500 in total, waited until their prices plummet up to the point that they were only worth $4 each, and then repurchased them — you would then have to return the 100 stocks at the end of the month, but you'd also get to keep the $100 profit.

Small company funds: These are mutual funds that exclusively invest in stocks belonging to companies that have a market capitalization of less than $500 million.

Target funds: These are mutual funds that exclusively invest in bonds that will all mature within the same year. They are called 'target' funds because they pay out profits to their investors in a 'target' year.

World bond funds: These are mutual funds that invest in local and international bonds.

World stock funds: These are mutual funds that invest in local and international stocks.

Stocks and the Stock Market: Easily Understandable Enigmas

Stocks (which are also called shares) are little pieces of companies that can be bought or sold through traditional or over-the-counter stock exchanges. Owning stocks in a company means that you own a "percentage" of that company's equities (for example, if you owned 100 stocks in a company which had only issued 500, you'd own 20% of the company's equity). This ownership entitles you to voting rights and a portion of any dividends which it may pay out. Some kinds of stocks also give their stockholders a measure of control over the company's profits or assets.

There are four different kinds of stocks: private stocks, public stocks, common stocks and preferred stocks.

Public stocks are the ordinary shares that most traders invest in. They are traded openly on the major stock exchanges, which means that anyone with sufficient capital can purchase them.

Private stocks are not traded over-the-counter or through any of the major stock exchanges. They are usually sold to investors who the company approaches with an offer of stocks in exchange for a capital investment. Private investors usually request a return on their investment, as well as a certain percentage of ownership in the company.

Investors who own preferred stock are not entitled to any voting rights, but they are guaranteed fixed dividend payments (which means that they receive regular, predictable payouts at predetermined intervals).

Shareholders who own common stock are entitled to voting rights and a portion of the company's profits in the form of variable dividends. However, common stocks' dividend payments are erratic and unpredictable both in timing and amount, and some companies never pay out any at all.

Preferred stockholders are in the best position in the event that the company the stocks belong to goes bankrupt because preferred stockholders are refunded first (alongside creditors and bondholders), this means that common stockholders are only refunded if there is any capital left after paying off the aforementioned parties.

Ninety-nine percent of all of the stocks which are bought and sold are common stocks. This means that your average investor doesn't have to be overly concerned about the advantages or disadvantages of preferred stock.

Companies sell stock in order to raise capital to reinvest back into their operations. Companies whose stocks perform well on the stock market are eligible for better loans and more credit, which means that companies' owners are encouraged to "go public" in order to secure a better financial future for their enterprises.

There are numerous ways to start investing in the stock market, the easiest of which are through your IRA or 401(k) account.

Many companies offer their employees the chance to invest a portion of their monthly wages into a 401(k) account. You are usually not able to invest in individual stocks through such an account, but you are likely to have a range of mutual funds to choose from. A 401(k) account is a brilliant way to invest in the stock market if you want absolutely nothing to do with the stock market, as most of them are managed entirely by a fund manager (which means that you, as the investor, have very little power over which stocks or funds are invested in, for how much, or when).

IRA accounts are the go-to option for those who would like a 401(k) account but who are self employed or whose employers don't offer this benefit. However, just because IRAs are less popular, that doesn't mean that they are less advantageous. In fact, one could argue that IRAs are the better option because they allow you to invest in a wide variety of mutual funds and individual stocks. IRAs also offer investors more control than traditional 401(k) accounts do because investors can choose to either manage their entire stock portfolio through their IRA themselves or they can make use of a robo-advisor to do it for them. An IRA is a better choice for someone who is looking to be actively involved in the trading process than a 401(k) account is.

Investors who would like to start trading stocks, but who don't wish to do so through one of the aforementioned accounts, need to open an investing account through an existing stock brokerage firm like Wealthfront or Ameritrade. Depending on the type of investment account, investors may need to set aside an additional sum of money to pay for its management, commission, trade, or annual fees. Luckily, in modernity, many stock brokerage firms have waived their fees entirely. Firms like Robinhood, Ameritrade, and Interactive Brokers all offer investment options which do not charge investors fees of any kind.

The History of the Stock Market: What We Can Learn From Our Mistakes

The Dutch East India Company's reputation has been (deservedly) ruined beyond repair because of its historical role in the propagation of slavery, but that doesn't mean that it didn't contribute anything worthwhile during its existence. The Dutch East Indian Company was the first company in the world to ever sell shares, and it had to help erect the Amsterdam Stock Exchange in order to do so. It had 'invented' this method of collecting money to sponsor its voyages after it became apparent that the dangers posed by Barbary pirates made a large enough investment from a single investor impossible, however, people were willing to take the risk if they only paid a portion of the voyage's costs in exchange for a percentage of any profits which might possibly result from the voyage.

This idea evolved over a decade or so and eventually led to the Dutch East India Company selling 'pieces' of itself instead of portions of planned voyages — historians believe that these first stocks were a fantastic investment that offered the company's investors a rate of return of nearly 16% every year. The fact that people were making money off of the shares issued by the Dutch East India Company led to the rise of this kind of investment's popularity.

About 80 years after the Dutch East India Company made its initial public offering, the first book to ever be written about stock trading was published. Its title was *Confusion of Confusions* and its author, Joseph de la Vega, warned his readers about the inherent volatility of the stock market and the correlating importance of being willing to invest for periods of 10 years or longer.

The first government bonds were invented by the English government another decade after the publication of *Confusion of Confusions*. The English government started this initiative as a way of raising money for its ever-ongoing wars. The idea was so well received that England's first stock markets started popping up a few years later.

Stock market fever soon swept over the globe, and in 1790 the United States of America saw the opening of its very own first stock market in Philadelphia. At the time it was called the "Board of Brokers" but it soon came to be known as the Philadelphia Stock Exchange. Despite being the first, it wasn't the most successful.

That title went to (and still goes to) the New York Stock Exchange (NYSE) which was founded under a buttonwood tree another decade later. It soon moved to its location on Wall Street where it remains to this day.

The rise of the stock market as we know it today didn't come without its challenges. Over the course of its more than 400 year long history, it has seen a number of crashes and recessions caused by a multitude of factors.

The first stock market crash happened in 1637 in the Netherlands and is known as the "tulip mania bubble." This bubble burst when the price of tulip future contracts, which had previously been feverishly traded on the Amsterdam Stock Exchange, suddenly sharply declined — leaving traders who had invested in these futures gasping for air. This bubble was caused by over-excitement amongst investors over the introduction of tulip futures to the stock market. A similar bear market had occurred in the Dutch stock market a few years earlier after shares in hyacinths devalued to nearly zero overnight. Investors either naively or ignorantly ignored the signs that tulip futures would go the route of hyacinth shares, and paid dearly when the market did inevitably crash.

The American stock market underwent its first major recession in 1907. This market crash can largely be attributed to sabotage. During the period leading up to this recession, the Knickerbocker Trust Company manipulated the value of stocks in copper companies through insider trading. United Copper suffered the most, nearly declaring bankruptcy. Investors started scooping up shares in the aforementioned company as it started to recover from its brush with bankruptcy. The optimism was short-lived however, as just as United Copper's share price started gaining momentum, it crashed again. This crash caused thousands of investors to panic and sell their stocks off by the hundreds — which, consequently, drove the stock market down even further. This incident led to the formation of the Federal Reserve a few years later, and imprinted the importance of market regulations on the American psyche. Although this was the first American stock market recession caused by investors panicking, it certainly wasn't the last.

In 1929, after a period of immense sustained growth, the Dow Jones Industrial Average fell by more than 12% in a single trading day. This depreciation was so unprecedented that the stock market's elementary ticker tape system couldn't keep up, which means that investors were deprived of the ability to see a stock's up to date sales and pricing information. Once again, investors panicked. Phone lines crashed and telegrams failed as traders scrambled to contact the various exchanges for current information of the shares held in their portfolios. This panic led to traders selling off most of their stocks, hoping to offload them before the imagined-apocalyptic recession devalued them even further. Of course, ironically, it was the fact that most investors were feverishly selling off their stocks that drove the stock market into a recession in the first place.

The American stock market crashed again 58 years later — and for much the same reason. The various American exchanges slowly devalued over a five-day period leading up to the nineteenth of October which finally saw the Dow Jones Industrial Average fall by more than 22% in a single trading day. Traders panicked, convinced that the long foretold market crash caused by overvaluation and program trading was upon them, and quickly sold off most of the shares held in their portfolios. The NYSE received so many sell orders on this fateful day in October that it had to halt trading numerous times in order to be able to process all of them. Once again, just as was the case in 1907 and 1929, this over-selling drove many companies' stocks' value down to nearly zero, leading to a sustained recession that plagued America for years.

The most recent American stock market crash occurred about 12 years ago in 2008. This year saw the collapse of 15 American banks largely due to irresponsible lending practices (loans were granted to people who would never have been able to pay them back). The collapse of these banks sent investors into a frenzy, and history once again repeated itself. The rapid high-cycling trading led to the devaluation of the stocks being traded and caused the Dow Jones Industrial Average to fall by more than 50% over just a bit more than a one year period.

All of the notable historic recessions were caused by the same thing: a negative herd mentality. When investors believe *"it's the end of the world"* for whatever reason, they seem to be willing to sell off their stocks for below-par prices in the hope of being able to line their apocalypse-bunkers with more cash. While it's always tempting to just follow the majority, history shows us that holding onto your stocks when times are the most uncertain is probably the best move to make. Panic-selling has never made anyone rich.

Getting to Know the Stock Exchanges You're Most Likely to Trade On

There are hundreds of stock exchanges operating around the world at any given moment, but it's highly unlikely that you'll interact with all of them. There are four major stock exchanges: the Nasdaq, the NYSE, the London Stock Exchange, and the Euronext.

Both the Nasdaq and the NYSE are located in New York City. This means that Americans have a distinct advantage when it comes to the accessibility of major stock exchanges.

The Nasdaq has a total market capitalization of approximately $10 trillion (that's $10,000,000,000,000 for perspective) and facilitates the trade of about $40 billion worth of stocks every day. The Nasdaq's name was initially an acronym for the 'National Association of Securities Dealers Automated Quotations' at its inception in 1971, however, it kept its name after its split from the National Association of Securities Dealers in 2000. The Nasdaq was originally a software system used to generate stock quotes, and then later started facilitating the trade of over-the-counter stocks. By 1981 it was facilitating the trade of more than a third of all American stock exchanges, and by 1987 it had become the United States' first online stock exchange. Within a matter of decades from its inception, it had managed to rise from its humble beginnings and had become the stock market giant we know it as today.

The NYSE is the largest stock exchange in the world. It has a market capitalization of $22 trillion (more than twice that of the second largest stock exchange in the world, the Nasdaq) and is responsible for facilitating the trade of more than $169 billion worth of stocks every day. It was formed in 1972 by the Buttonwood Agreement after 24 stockbrokers agreed to make a space available for traders to meet and conduct trades at for a fee.

The London Stock Exchange (LSE) has a market capitalization of about $4.5 trillion and facilitates the trade of about $219 billion worth of stocks every month. The LSE houses stocks from 2,600 different companies with over 60 different nationalities It started off as the Royal Exchange which was formed in 1571 by Queen Elizabeth I, but initially did not allow stock traders into the building that housed it because they were considered noisy and rude against the standards of the time. It was only after it burned down during the Great Fire of London that it started taking on some of the characteristics which it still has today.

Euronext facilitates the trade of about $174 billion worth of stocks every month and has a market capitalization of about $3,9 trillion. Its name was originally an acronym for "European New Exchange Technology." Unlike the Nasdaq and the NYSE, Euronext doesn't just consist of one singular central exchange, instead it operates a number of exchanges located in Oslo, Paris, Amsterdam, Brussels, London, Dublin, and Lisbon. Euronext was created in 2000 by the merging of the then Amsterdam Stock Exchange, Paris Bourse, and Brussels Stock Exchange.

The kind of stocks you're interested in investing in will determine which of the major stock exchanges you'll trade through.

Stock Prices: Why They Go Up and Why They Go Down

Just as is the case with any other commodity, stocks' prices are determined by their underlying supply and demand. If the demand for them is high but they're low in supply — they'll be expensive. If the demand for them is low and they're abundant — they'll be cheap. Of course, it's a little more complicated than that.

Inflation, which affects the price of everything over time, also causes stock prices to gradually increase. In the 1960s you could get a milkshake, fries, and a burger for about 45 cents, today the same meal will cost you about six dollars — that's inflation in action. Investors who buy long position stocks (stocks which they plan on owning for many years) often profit on their sale largely due to the effect of inflation on their prices.

A stock's price is also largely determined by the well-being of the sector it belongs to, which means that positive market sentiment over its sector moves its price up, while negative market sentiment has the opposite effect. An example of this would be a negative market sentiment towards oil companies after an international meeting on climate change driving the price of shares in Royal Dutch Shell down.

The price of a stock can also be influenced by the type of person which its average investor is. This might sound far-fetched, but stocks that attract older investors tend to have lower stock prices as these kinds of investors often sell their shares in order to finance their retirements (and as we know, increased sales volume drives down a stock's price). On the other hand, stocks whose main investors are middle aged tend to be higher in value because these kinds of investors are more likely to invest in long position stocks.

The news (inter-corporational, local, national, and international) also has a profound effect on a stock's price. If one of the heads of a company is caught in the middle of a scandal (including anything from an extra-marital affair to fraud), that company's stock price may suffer despite the operations or profitability of the company not necessarily being affected. Similarly, news of a drought may cause traders to abandon their investments in an agricultural company, while news of a large-scale suburban fire might drive up the stock price of building material companies (as the demand for their products increases).

Stock market analysts would like to believe that they can predict a stock's future price through fundamental and technical analysis, but the truth is that if any prediction system was entirely accurate, there would be many more stock market millionaires in the world than there currently are.

Chapter 2:

What You Need To Know

Before Entering This Next

Level

Once you're confident that you understand the basic mechanisms behind stock trading, you need to decide what kind of trader you'd like to be, as this will determine the kind of strategy you will employ and how much research you'll need to do in selecting stocks for your portfolio.

Some people prefer to be passive investors, others choose to be active investors. Passive investors aren't interested in trying to beat the market by rapidly up-selling stocks, they would just like a nice solid 10- to 15-year investment that will reliably grow over time and that offers them a predictable rate of return. The fact that they aren't interested in managing their portfolios themselves means that they often make use of funds (that are managed by fund managers) or robo-advisors. Both of the aforementioned options allow them to put down their money and walk away, only to return at a later date basically guaranteed that their investment would have grown. Active investors are a bit more open to taking risks and are generally more interested in high-cycle trading, this also means that they normally don't want someone buying and selling stocks on their behalf as they'd prefer to perform this function themselves. Consequently, active investors tend to shy away from funds, stock advisors, and robo-advisors.

There is no 'right' way to invest in the stock market. Passive investors are just as likely to meet their financial goals as active investors are. The only reason why it is important to classify yourself as either is to help you to make choices regarding your investments.

Many stock traders make use of both strategies at different points in their lives, and then stick with the one that they believe was most profitable. Although experimentation is never a bad thing (don't tell your teenagers!), you shouldn't choose a trading style based on the one that you think generates the largest sum of cash. You should choose the trading style that best fits your lifestyle and personality. If you're an aggressive workaholic that likes to micromanage, you should be an active trader. If you're a laid-back person, or you're prone to anxiety, and you'd prefer to do as little as possible — you should be a passive trader. If your trading style doesn't suit your personality, you'll soon find yourself becoming burned-out and discouraged.

Once you've categorized yourself, you need to make an effort to understand the economy's effect on the stock market, and from there onwards you can start drawing up a budget, choosing a strategy, and researching stocks.

The Economy: The Magical Driving Force Behind the Stock Market

The economy consists of all of the assets bought and sold, and all of the services delivered, in a specific area. When we talk about the economy, we're usually referring to the financial status of a specific country. A country's economy is usually quantified through its gross domestic product (GDP). Countries usually measure their GPDs using a formula based on the countries expenses. The formula looks like this:

Government spending + net exports + investments + consumption = GDP

The United States of America boasts the largest GDP in the world, followed by China, Japan, Germany, and the United Kingdom (in that order). Tuvalu, Nauru, and Kiribati have the smallest GDPs in the world (which isn't surprising when you consider that Tuvalu and Nauru have populations of less than 13,000, while Birikati has a population of only 116,000).

Once you know that the economy is measured by the government's performance, it becomes easy to understand why the government might meddle in the stock market by trying to give it an artificial boost. One of the ways that the American government has rejuvenated the stock market over the years is through what can only be described as war-enthusiasm, and it's not a new concept. Economists have known for decades that economies benefit from international war (however, this is not the case with civil wars). World War I and World War II saw the American stock market experience a 115% boom, although America isn't the only country whose economy has historically benefitted from violent conflicts. Korea and Japan's economies both grew by more than 10% following the Korean War and World War II. Times of war and conflict have also historically been times of invention and ingenuity — modern aircraft, the computer, and nuclear energy were all originally invented to serve an offensive or defensive purpose during wartime, and it's no different in modernity. When a company is actively engaged in an international conflict many of its economic sectors receive a boost because of their necessity too; war increases the demand for oil, for steel, for ammunition and guns, for vehicles, for safety equipment, and for medical technology. Not only is war a fantastic consumer, but it also creates jobs as the military scrambles to sufficiently fill its ranks and as the companies who are contracted to provide goods and services are forced to expand their operations to keep up with demand. While it might be a moral gray area, it's understandable why governments might want to keep up their engagements in international conflict (either by 'liberating' countries from dictators, or by warring with terrorists, or through getting involved with one of the United Nations' international peace-keeping operations).

Of course, war is just an example of one of the most extreme techniques that a government might employ in order to aid its national stock market. Governments have also been known to purposely inflate their countries' currencies, decrease financial institutions' inflation rates through legislation, and subsidize (or bailout) entire industries using taxpayers' money in order to help their stock markets perform optimally.

Despite the government's engagement with the stock market, its role in the economy is largely limited to the sphere of macroeconomics.

The study of the economy can be broken down into two further subsections: microeconomics and macroeconomics. Microeconomics is concerned with the purchasing and investment choices of individuals, while macroeconomics is concerned with the study of economics in its entirety.

Modern microeconomics is largely based on the general equilibrium theory which was first posited by Léon Walras (a French mathematical economist) in 1874. This theory states that all economic sectors tend towards equilibrium — this means that all economic sectors have a tendency to generate an amount of demand that is equal to the amount of supply that they create. The result of this theory in action is that sectors that increase their supply indirectly also increase their demand, while the inverse is also true.

Modern macroeconomics isn't as straight-forward as microeconomics is. It is divided into a number of different schools of thought, namely: monetarist, classical, Keynesian, Austrian, and neoclassical. The monetarist school of thought was founded by Milton Friedman (an American economist who received a Nobel Memorial Prize for his work) and believes that the supply of money in a country should be controlled and throttled by the government in order to thwart the damaging effects of inflation. The classical school of thought is largely based on the teachings of Adam Smith and holds that the government should not regulate the supply of money or legislate economic activities within a country's economy as it believes that healthy economies are self-regulating. The Keynesian school of thought (named after its creator John Maynard Keynes) holds that the government should control private economic activities to some degree through monetary and fiscal policies in order to prohibit or circumvent the formation of market monopolies. The Austrian school of thought states that, when considering the unpredictability of human economic activities, government intervention in the finances or operations of privately-owned businesses is futile. Finally, the neoclassical school of thought is similar to the microeconomic's general equilibrium theory in the sense that it believes that the larger economy is naturally in constant equilibrium —

constantly (and without guidance) adjusting its supply and demand in order to remain in balance.

The stock market and the economy are connected in many ways. Generally speaking, if the stock market is doing well the economy will be doing well too, and vice versa. Stock markets tend to operate best in market-based economies, for this reason, stock traders are usually more invested in the Austrian and classical economic ideologies. Many countries' governments encourage their citizens to actively invest in the stock market as an increase in investment has the potential to give any economy a boost. Stock market analysts keep an eye on the economy in order to determine the best times to buy and sell stock. It's best to buy stocks when the economy is struggling and to sell them when it's booming, while buying while it's booming and selling in a recession is a recipe for bankruptcy.

How to Research Stocks So That You Don't End Up Investing In Duds

Before you start researching individual stocks to invest in, you should decide whether you want to invest in growth stocks or value stocks. Growth stocks are shares that investors invest in because they hope that their value will increase over a period of time so that when they sell them they can profit off of their capital appreciation. Value stocks are shares that investors invest in because they make regular, sizable dividend payments to their shareholders. Active traders tend to prefer investing in growth stocks which they can buy and sell over a course of minutes, hours, or day. Passive traders normally prefer value stocks because they're profitable even if you just buy them and allow them to stagnate in your portfolio for a couple of years.

The best way to start researching stocks is by reading other stock market analysts' reports. Some of the most helpful online analyst reports can be found through Zacks Investment Research, Seeking Alpha, Morningstar, AAII Stock Screens, Barron's, and MarketWatch. Reading the research done by more experienced analysts can help you to cut a few corners by pointing you in the right direction instead of leaving you to sift through mountains of raw data all by yourself. Of course, you shouldn't base your decision to invest in any particular stock solely based on the opinion of some anonymous blogger, you need to do your own research in order to be sure that you're making a good investment.

Knowing where to start your research is half the battle. Some traders make use of a top-down strategy which involves looking into the potential of individual companies before considering the financial well being of the economic sector that they belong to, while other traders make use of a bottom-down strategy which involves considering the prosperity of the stock's economic sector before even glimpsing at data pertaining to individual stocks.

Regardless of which strategy you choose to use, the most difficult part is researching individual stocks themselves. The simplest starting point is reviewing the stock's holding company's annual report. Companies that trade publicly on any of the major American stock exchanges are obligated by law to provide interested parties with a full record of their financial, operational, and management performance and goals. This annual report usually consists of a description of the company's operations, details pertaining to any relevant legal proceedings, a summary of risk factors, financial data represented in graphs and charts, and finally discussions penned by the company's executive heads on its financial outlook and possible challenges.

The section of an annual report dedicated to legal proceedings is perhaps one of the most pertinent pieces of the document, but is often overlooked. Investors need to keenly consider any lawsuits pending against companies that they're considering investing in as losing a large lawsuit can bankrupt even some of the most prolific companies around. Naturally, you should also comb over the company's cash flow statements (which can be found in the company's annual report's "financial details" section). Companies with a lot of money coming in and going out of their accounts daily tend to be better investment options because this is a sign of healthy trade, while companies whose only assets are long term assets, and whose only expenses are debts, are best left alone.

You can analyze the well-being of the economic sector which a stock belongs to by keeping an eye on the values of sector specific funds. For example, if the Financial Select Sector SPDR ETF is trading well, you know that the financial sector is also performing well, whereas if the Fidelity Select Technology Fund is trading well, traders can assume that the technology sector is also blossoming.

Smart traders also determine which stocks to invest in by examining stocks' earnings per share (EPS). Companies usually make this value available to the general public in their annual report. This value is calculated by taking a company's annual profits and dividing them by the number of shares the company has issued. Companies with higher EPS values tend to sell their shares for higher prices, and thus are better investments.

Some stock market analysts use a company's EPS value to calculate another value which they believe predicts the success of a stock — its price-to-earnings ratio (P/E ratio). This value is determined by taking a stock's price and dividing it by its holding company's EPS value. Analysts believe that a lower P/E ratio is indicative of a promising stock. However, technical analysts are often unsatisfied with the accuracy of a company's P/E ratio in relation to its performance. This has led to some leaning more heavily on an analytical value called the price-to-earnings growth ratio (PEG ratio). PEG ratio is calculated by taking a stock's P/E ratio and dividing it by the company's growth over a one year period. Investors who believe in the predictive powers of PEG ratios hold that companies with a PEG ratio of less than one are better investments.

It's important to keep the kind of company you'd like to invest in in mind when choosing stocks to buy. If you're an active trader, you're likely better off considering stocks belonging to up-and-coming companies that have the potential to significantly increase in value as their holding companies grow. If you're a passive trader, you should focus your energy on stocks belonging to well-established blue chip companies that regularly make sizable dividend payments to their investors and whose stocks slowly (but predictably) increase in value over time.

Budgets Are Boring, But They're Important

If you want to live like Jordan Belfort did in the *Wolf of Wall Street* (or any other successful Wall Street trader), budgeting might seem a tad bit 'uncool', but it is, unfortunately, a necessity. Don't let the wealthy fool you, they might not be counting pennies but that doesn't mean that they're not keeping track of how much money they're spending and on what. Nobody has ever become a millionaire by disregarding their finances entirely.

The first financial factor you'll need to consider before investing in the stock market is that you need capital in order to structure a diversified portfolio that has a real shot at succeeding. Many online stock brokerages offer trading accounts with no minimum investment requirements — this means that it might be tempting to start investing with very little initial capital, but you should reconsider. Although it is entirely possible to start investing with just $10 to your name, it's not a smart investment move. As an aspiring-millionaire your stock portfolio should be watertight from the get-go, this means that it needs to be diversified enough to consist of stocks belonging to a number of economic sectors, as well as investments in mutual funds or ETFs. Diversification is simply not possible if you only have $100 to spend (considering that shares in a company like Amazon might cost you more than $2,000 per share). Ideally, you should aim to save up at least $1,000 before you approach any brokerage firms or open an investment account.

The first step to saving up enough money to finance your investment in the stock market is to decrease the amount of money which you spend every month. This is a pretty tall order when you consider the fact that most Americans live paycheck to paycheck, but it is possible for everyone regardless of their income level.

You don't have to save thousands of dollars every month in order to finance your stock trading dreams, in fact if you can manage to save $83 a month for an entire year you would have saved up enough to make your first $1,000 investment.

There are a number of ways to cut down on your monthly expenses (although admittedly none of them are much fun) — you could opt to make use of public transport more often, you could avoid spending money at takeaway joints and restaurants by choosing to cook at home instead (preparing meals from scratch is much cheaper than buying a ready-made meal), or you could choose to purchase generic and store-name brand instead of name brands (as they're usually much cheaper too).

Fortunately, living in the cyber-age offers investors some nifty money-saving and financial management mechanisms in the form of software applications ('apps'). One of the best apps to download if you're struggling to keep up with your expenses is called 'Mint.' This application connects your bank accounts to a central database (don't worry, it's super secure) and keeps records of your income and expenses. It uses the information it gathers from this to generate graphs depicting what you're spending the most money on every month and to suggest a budget to you. You should definitely consider downloading it if you're someone that struggles to keep your purchasing habits under control.

Another fantastic financial application to consider downloading is called Qapital (which is available for iOS and Android). This application rounds every transaction that you make up to the nearest dollar and then deposits the difference into an FDIC-insured account. Scraping cents together might not sound like the fastest way to save $1,000, but you'd be surprised how quickly it all adds up. For example, if you bought an iced coffee on your way to work for $3.45, got an uber and paid its fare of $8.25, bought a burger and fries for $6.10 for lunch, and then later purchased a packet of cigarettes for $7.80 on your way home, you would have saved $2.40 without even noticing it.

You might be tempted to dip into your "rainy day fund" or your retirement account in order to generate the capital you need to fund your investments in the stock market, but you should think twice before using money which you had originally put away for other purposes (like your children's college fund). Why? Because the risk that you could lose all of the money you had invested in the stock market is ever present. The risk might be small, but it's never zero. You should only be investing money in the stock market that you're prepared to lose.

You should also avoid investing more than 10% of your investment money in individual stocks. I know this might seem disheartening to those of you that were hoping to handpick your entire portfolio, but it's simply just a bad idea. At least 90% of your portfolio should consist of investments in mutual funds and ETFs.

Individual stocks are more likely to fail and lose all of their value because individual companies are more likely to face bankruptcy. Mutual funds and ETFs consist of stocks belonging to numerous different companies (sometimes hundreds of different companies), this means that even if one (or two) of them goes bankrupt the fund can still continue to operate and may even manage to remain profitable.

Of course, not all mutual funds and ETFs were created equally. While many try to keep their costs low in order to attract investors, some charge exorbitant commission and annual fees. The bulk of your portfolio should consist of low-cost, broad based mutual funds and ETFs as these will keep your annual costs low and will ensure a steady flow of returns throughout the year. The Schwab S&P 500 Index is probably the best fund to invest in if you're looking to get value for your money. It only charges about $0.2 for every $1,000 you invest and has no required minimum investment amount, despite being one of the more economical choices it has been able to supply its investors with a steady rate of income for many years. The Fidelity NASDAQ Composite Index and the Schwab International Index Fund are also good choices (and just like The Schwab S&P 500 Index, they have no required minimum investment amount). The Fidelity NASDAQ Composite Index only charges about $3 for every $1,000 you invest while the Schwab International Index Fund only costs approximately $0.6 for every $1,000 invested. Both of these funds have fantastic reputations and serve as the core investment in many successful stock traders' portfolios.

You Might Consider Yourself A Rebel, But You May Need to Follow Some Trends

A market trend is defined as the stock market's propensity to move upwards or downwards. Being able to predict them helps stock traders to know when to buy stocks and when to sell them (as it is best to buy them when the stock market is bearish and to sell them when it is bullish).

Market trends fall into one of three categories: secular, primary, and secondary. Secular market trends, which are made up of a bunch of smaller primary market trends, are long term market trends and last for anything between five years and a quarter of a century. They can further be subdivided into secular bear market trends and secular bull market trends. Secular bear market trends are defined by the stock market's prolonged period of downward trajectory, while secular bull market trends are characterized by the stock market's prolonged growth.

Primary market trends last for anything between one and five years and secondary markets last for a number of weeks or months. Both can also be subdivided into bull and bear categories.

Market trends are caused by a number of factors, namely governmental policies, international trade, supply and demand, and speculation.

Just as is the case with the economy (as was discussed earlier), the government can alter the stock market's trajectory by adjusting the country's inflation and by lowering interest rates across the board.

International transactions affect market trends in a number of ways. Firstly, international companies are often directly in competition with national companies, which means that their growth is directly correlated with local losses. International trade also affects the stock market on a macroeconomic level in the sense that an increase in importation can cripple a local stock market (as money which could have been spent locally leaves the country's borders) while exportation can help an economy to grow, which in turn is responsible for the growth of the local stock market.

Speculation is how investors feel the stock market is doing. It's not necessarily based in reality, but it can affect stock prices nonetheless. For example, if the vast majority of stock investors were hoping that a Republican candidate wins the election, but a Democrat wins it instead, the stock market may start declining based on nothing but the investors' belief that it will decline under the newly elected president. The problem with speculation is that it's incredibly hard to quantify or study because it's not based on any corporeal factors. The only way investors can really hope to stay abreast of trends based on speculation is by keenly following the news, keeping up to date with analyst reports, and by communicating with their fellow stock traders.

Supply and demand may also affect stock market trends as periods of increased demand are responsible for bullish periods, while an oversupply of stocks or decrease in demand is usually (at least partially) responsible for bearish periods. Supply and demand is largely determined by the well-being of the economy. When the economy is doing well and unemployment figures are low, a bigger portion of the general public has enough money to invest in the stock market, which means the demand for stocks increases. The opposite is true when the economy is struggling or unemployment figures are high, as this means that there are fewer potential stock market investors, which in turn leads to a decrease in demand.

Knowing When to Buy and When to Sell

Being aware of stock market trends but being unable to interpret or predict them is pretty useless. Investors use stock market trends to know when to buy new stocks and when to sell some of the stocks already held in their portfolios. As the late Kenny Rogers said, "you've got to know when to hold 'em and know when to fold 'em."

One of the simplest ways to analyze the stock market is by staying up to date with the Commodity Futures Trading Commission's Commitments of Traders report. This report is a compilation of all of the futures trades made by institutional investors. The reason why this is a nifty resource is that it separates professionals' trading data from your average Joe's trading data, which will give you a clearer image of the overall market sentiment as institutional investors usually trade much larger volumes of stocks (and for much steeper profits).

Another easy way to gather data on the stock market's trajectory is by reviewing stock market indicators. There are a number of online indicators out there that are incredibly reliable, though I specifically recommend JPMorgan's Global Manufacturing Purchasing Managers' Index and ISM's Manufacturing Report On Business. JPMorgan's Global Manufacturing Purchasing Managers' Index tracks the trading choices of a small number of top institutional investors from all around the world, while ISM's Manufacturing Report On Business only tracks the purchasing habits of American institutional investors. It's always a good idea to try and make your investments mirror those of brokers from the world's top stock brokerage firms.

Once you've determined that market trends indicate that it's the right time to buy stocks, it's time to start searching for undervalued stocks to invest in. Undervalued stocks are stocks that are selling for less than they're intrinsically valued, this means that their stock price has the potential to skyrocket once investors realize that they're missing out. Undervalued stocks all have five characteristics in common: low market-to-book ratios, high dividend yields, low relative price performances, and low P/E ratios. A company's market-to-book ratio is a value derived from comparing the price of its stocks to their actual value, while you'll know that its price performance is low if its stocks are selling for less than the average sum which other shares from the same economic sector are selling. We discussed P/E ratios and their relevance a bit earlier in the chapter — a low P/E ratio indicates that you can expect to earn more for every penny you invest in a stock, this means that it's almost always indicative of a good investment choice.

Knowing when to sell stocks already held in your portfolio is a little bit trickier, although there is a four-pronged rule that you can apply in order to help you make the decision. This rule states that you should sell your stocks if you need to withdraw funds from your portfolio in order to spend them on a better investment, if the stock's holding company is acquired by or merged with a different company that you do not approve of for whatever reason, if the reasons which originally motivated your purchase of the stocks have changed, or if you need to rearrange your portfolio in order to improve its diversification.

If you're investing in growth stocks, you should also attempt to sell shares just as their stock price peaks. This happens after a period of frenzied buying which dramatically increases the stock's price over a period of days or weeks. The reason why you should sell stocks before they peak is that their prices drastically decline again thereafter as all of the investors who bought-in during the frenzied scramble to offload their shares before their prices inevitably crash. You can determine whether a stock is on an upwards trajectory, moving towards peaking, by examining its relative strength index (RSI). RSI is measured in a figure ranging from 1 to 100. This figure represents the momentum of the stock's sales. Stocks with RSI below 30 are set to steadily increase in value. The closer this value comes to 30, the closer the stock is to peaking. Once a stock's RSI value is above 30, it has already peaked and is starting to devalue again. There are a number of free RSI indicators available online, one of the simplest to use can be found on Tradeview's website (tradeview.com).

There are also dates and times that are literally better for buying and selling stocks. Stock prices fluctuate the most during the first and last hours of the trading day (in other words, from 9 a.m. to 10 a.m., and then again from 3 p.m. to 4 p.m.). This means that these two hours are the ideal time for investors to buy and sell stocks if they're hoping to profit off of marginal differences in the stock's price from the beginning of the trading day till its end.

The best days on which to buy stocks are Mondays and Thursdays. Just like the Boomtown Rats, stock investors don't like Mondays. This means that the stock market takes a dip on Mondays as fewer stocks are sold and the level of demand is minimal. In fact, shares belonging to the S&P 500 Index fall by an average of 0.2% on Mondays. The same is true for Thursdays (which also see an average decline of 0.2% across the board). Analysts speculate that Thursdays are responsible for this reduction in value because it is the day that stock traders choose to offload stocks in order to free up money for the upcoming weekend. Regardless of the reasons behind these twice-weekly stock market dips, they're a fantastic opportunity to scoop up shares for lower-than-usual prices (which in turn makes it easier to profit off of the eventual sale of these shares).

The best day to sell stocks on is Friday, the beginning of the weekend. Analysts aren't entirely sure why the stock market tends to do so well on Fridays, though they suspect that people's excitement over the weekend makes them more likely to buy stocks at higher prices. The stock market tends to grow by about 0.14% on Fridays. This might sound like an insignificant amount to you, but it really adds up if you're trading a large volume of stocks.

The best months to buy stocks in are May and September, as historical patterns show us that the stock market experiences its steepest declines during these months, while the best months to sell stocks in are January and December, as this is when the stock market offers the highest returns (this means that stock prices will also be at all all-time high).

When it comes to knowing when to buy or sell stocks, you should always keep the stock market's golden rule in mind: buy low and sell high. You should always aim to invest in the stock market when stock prices are at their lowest, and if part of your investment strategy is the regular sale of stocks held within your portfolio you need to aim to sell them when stock prices are at their highest.

Floor Traders, Exchange Specialists, And The Dangers of Inside Trading

There are a number of people pulling the stock market's strings behind the scenes, this means that when it comes to trading your success might largely be determined not by what you know, but by who you know. It's important that, at the very least, you're aware of these internal forces' presence — though ideally, you'd also try to befriend them and become part of the inner circle.

In the past it was easy to befriend some of the country's top traders by visiting the stock exchange's 'pit' (an area located on the stock exchange's trading floor dedicated to the trading of a certain type of security). You may have seen examples of stock exchange pits on movies like Floored. They're usually depicted as bustling sales floors full of hundreds of traders screaming either "buy!" or "sell!" — pushing and shoving to improve their position. While this has never been an entirely accurate depiction, it is true that pits once used to accommodate hundreds of traders from all around the country at once on any given trading day. This means that traders who were looking to make some powerful friends could do so merely by lurking in these pits and striking up conversations with some of the top investors. It's a bit trickier getting to know the country's best traders and brokers today because most trades are conducted electronically, which means that the days of traders being packed like sardines into pits are history.

Although stock exchange pits are mere shadows of their glorious past selves, they're still a good place to make some new connections. In today's times these pits are largely filled with floor traders. Floor traders (also known as individual liquidity providers) are individual stock traders who have passed a special screening process (which usually involves anything from a written test to fingerprints or a recommendation) that buy and sell stocks from a stock exchange's pit. Stock exchanges like the Milan Stock Exchange and London Stock Exchange have done away with floor traders altogether, opting to use automated systems instead, however, American stock exchanges have largely stuck with tradition as both the NYSE and the Chicago Mercantile Exchange still host floor traders who are physically located in their pits. Visiting these pits with the intention of covertly making 'friends' with one of the bigwigs who trades there isn't a bad idea. The more successful a floor trader is, the more successful friends (in the form of analysts and brokers) he or she will have. Befriending someone like this allows you to tap into their social circle, and possibly gain some inside knowledge.

There are a number of other clever ways to make powerful stock trading friends. Other than physically visiting the stock exchange, one of the simplest may be joining a local investment group. Investment groups are social groups composed of avid stock market investors.

A quick Google search of your area's name and "investment groups" should bring up tens (if not hundreds) of options. These groups are normally filled with traders from all walks of life, from the school teacher who is using his or her savings to buy two or three shares in Tesla, to the stock market millionaire who is wondering whether to offload 10,000 shares in Apple today or tomorrow. Both of these individuals are valuable people to know if you're looking to broaden your horizons, improve your perspective, and understand the stock market on a deeper level. Knowing the stock market millionaire's next trading moves might be helpful to you as you can mimic them and replicate the millionaire's profits. Knowing the school teacher is important because his or her trading choices will give you insight into the market sentiment of your average working class American (a group of people that make up the majority of investors in the stock market). Joining a physical investment group that meets once or twice a week isn't everybody's cup of tea — some suffer from social anxiety and some simply don't have the time. Luckily there is a workable alternative: online investment groups. One of the best online investment groups to join belongs to Bettertrade. Online investment groups arguably have even more benefits than physical investment clubs do because they allow you to connect with investors from across the country (in fact, it may even offer you the opportunity to mingle with international investors).

It's always good to have someone in your corner if you're in the business of trading stocks and stocks holding companies know this too. Unfortunately, having enough connections in the stock market can tempt any trader to engage in an array of market manipulation techniques, but you need to be careful — not all market manipulation techniques are legal (in fact most of them are frowned upon if they're not downright illegal).

Some of the most prevalent illegal market manipulation techniques are spoofing, layering, washing, churning, bear raiding (also known as "cornering the market"), painting the tape, shorting and distorting, front running, and insider trading.

Spoofing is when you place an order to sell a large number of stocks belonging to a certain company for below their market value, only to cancel the order before it is actioned. Doing so artificially deflates the stock's trading price as it causes other investors viewing its trading statistics to believe that it is naturally devaluing. Traders may engage in this illegal manipulation technique in hopes of driving down a stock's price in order to scoop up a large number of the same stock at a discounted price later on.

Layering is essentially the opposite of spoofing. It involves a trader placing an order to sell a large number of stocks belonging to a specific company for well-above their market price, only to cancel it before it is executed. Just as is the case with spoofing, doing so distorts the stock's trading statistics. This, in turn, leads to investors believing that a stock is worth more than it actually is. Crafty traders may make use of this technique to artificially boost a stock's trading price before selling off a number of stocks that they own in the affected company. Michael Coscia was found guilty of layering in 2013 after making use of a computer program which was programmed to place artificial sell orders and to hastily cancel them once placed in order to drive up a number of stocks' prices. A charge of layering or spoofing carries a maximum penalty of up to ten years' imprisonment or a fine of $1 million in the United States of America. However, Michael Coscia wasn't only tried by the U.S. Commodity Futures Trading Commission, he was also tried by Britain's Financial Conduct Authority who fined him and his firm a further $900,000.

Wash trading is when a trader sells stocks to him- or herself (and thus buys stocks from him- or herself) in order to manipulate the stock's trading statistics to reflect that it has a much higher trading volume than it actually has. The company Montgomery Street was accused of wash trading in 2014 after it sold stocks to itself in an attempt to raise a certain stock's price in the hope that it would attract more investors to its firm.

Your average stock trader doesn't have to be too concerned about committing a churning related offense because it is a market manipulation technique that can only be committed by brokers who are earning commissions off of clients' trades. Churning is when a broker sells and re-buys a large number of stocks held within a client's portfolio in order to increase the amount of commission that he can charge for managing the client's account.

A bear raid (also known as the 'short and distort' technique) is when a trader (or traders) intentionally drive down a stock's price by spreading malicious rumors in order to make a short selling deal which they had entered into more profitable. Bear raids have been a part of the stock market's landscape since its inception. The first bear raid occurred in 1609 after an investor named Isaac Le Maire forcefully drove down the Dutch East India Company's stock price. A more recent bear raid occurred in 2000 after an investor named Mark Jakob started spreading rumors that Emulex's chief executive officer (CEO) was about to resign. Of course, these rumors were entirely unfounded, and Mark Jakob had only been spreading them in order to profit off of a short selling deal that he had made on the stock at an earlier date. He managed to make about $240,000 by artificially driving down Emulex's share price, but didn't get to enjoy it by splurging it on a tropical holiday as he was caught and arrested shortly thereafter.

Painting the tape requires a certain level of teamwork. This makes it one of the more rarely seen forms of market fraud as it requires a great deal of collusion from the participating parties. It occurs when a number of traders start buying stocks from, and selling stocks to, each other in order to drive up their prices. Once they've artificially inflated these stocks' prices, they sell them off en masse at their newly adjusted prices to unsuspecting buyers — pocketing the difference.

The market manipulation technique known as "front running" occurs when brokers buy or sell stocks because they know their prices are about to go up or down. They know this because they themselves facilitated a large volume trade of that specific stock for a client that influenced its price. Front running is a type of insider trading. The American government is incredibly serious about preventing and cracking down on front running. In 2018 a currency broker named Mark Johnson was sentenced to two years in prison and fined an additional $300,000 by a District Court in New York for front-running after illegally benefitting from a client's $3.5 billion which saw the price of the British pound rally upwards.

The most well-known form of market manipulation is insider trading. Insider trading is when an individual or institutional trader buys or sells stocks based on confidential information that is not yet available to the general public. The most well-publicized case of insider trading is that of Martha Stewart. Martha Stewart was imprisoned in a Federal Prison in Alderson, West Virginia, for five months in 2004 after she was found guilty of having committed this form of market manipulation. This came after she sold all of the shares she had owned in a pharmaceutical company named ImClone in 2001 only to have its price fall by 16% 48-hours later. Authorities became suspicious and found during their investigation that Martha had known that

ImClone's new cancer treatment drug, Erbitux, had been rejected by the U.S. Food and Drug Administration (FDA) two days prior to the company announcing this rejection to the public, and that she had sold off the remainder of her shares in ImClone based on this confidential information. Insider trading has been a concern since long before Martha Stewart's case was heard. Robert Foster Winan (who wrote under the pen name 'R. Foster Winan') was a well-known Wall Street columnist who wrote the column known as "Heard on the Street." This column was so popular that the opinions which Robert expressed therein caused certain stock prices to increase or decrease. It wasn't long before Robert and his trader buddies realized that they could use this to their advantage. Robert started leaking his columns to traders before they were published so that they could base their investment decisions on Robert's readers' future reactions. Of course, this didn't go unnoticed, and led to Robert being convicted of insider trading in 1985.

It's always good to have influential friends if you're investing in the stock market, but it's important to stay on the right side of the law, regardless of how tempted you might be to use any confidential information that they might give you to improve your standing. There's no point in making $100,000 off of illegal trade, only to be sent to prison for two years and fined an additional $300,000. Our aim is to get you onto that yacht in the Bahamas, and you'll never be further away from that than when you're sitting behind bars.

Chapter 3:

Advanced Trading

Strategies

Unfortunately, successfully investing in the stock market isn't as easy as simply buying and selling stocks when and where your gut feeling tells you to — you need to have a plan, a strategy.

Luckily there are myriad strategies to choose from, and there's enough variety to accommodate every kind of investor. As mentioned earlier, you should choose a strategy that will be best suited to your lifestyle — your choice shouldn't be based on which one you think will help you to afford that yacht sooner.

Why Day Trading Isn't Just For Those Who Are Afraid of the Dark

Day trading is a stock trading strategy that involves buying shares at the stock market's open, only to sell them again some time before its close. Day traders make a profit by trading a large number of stocks at once and exploiting small differences in their prices throughout the day. For example, a day trader might buy 10,000 shares for $30 each, and sell them all three hours later for $31 each, making a profit of $10,000 with very little effort. While it might sound like a magical way to get rich quickly, it's not that simple. You need quite a substantial amount of start-up capital in order to start day trading because the entire strategy depends on your ability to trade a large number of stocks at once (this means that you need enough money to buy hundreds or thousands of shares at once). You also need to be able to accurately spot stocks which are about to experience a short term increase in value.

Jesse Lauriston Livermore, the founding father of day trading, was born in 1877 in Massachusetts in the United States of America. Livermore was born into extreme poverty and ran away from home at the age of 14, but that didn't stop him from being one of the richest people in the world later in his life. He made his first money off of the stock market at the age of 15 at a bucket shop along the Quincy and Burlington railroad where he bet $5 on a stock's performance. The bet went his way and he ended up winning back his $5 plus an additional $3.12. From there onwards, Livermore was hooked. He made his first big trade on the stock market at the age of 24 in 1901 after he managed to buy stocks in Northern Pacific Railway for $10,000 which he managed to sell a short time later for $500,000. At his peak, Livermore was worth about $1.5 billion (taking inflation into consideration). Livermore started actively trading stocks by building his portfolio at the beginning of the trading day and clearing it by the end during a time in which accurate up-to-date stock quotes and statistics were few and far between. He made his trades based on trends that he observed were taking place in the stock market, and executed them with shocking accuracy.

Despite Livermore's resounding success on the stock market, it didn't come without a cost. You see, day trading is a fantastic way to make a lot of money very quickly — but it's also an incredibly efficient way to lose your entire investment in the blink of an eye. Livermore lost everything due to bad trades about four times over the course of his life. Livermore went bankrupt for the last time in 1934 at the age of 56, although the exact cause of his bankruptcy remains unknown, it is clear that some kind of trading catastrophe caused him to lose all of his financial investments. Luckily, he had been smart enough to squirrel away millions into trust funds which allowed him and his wife to live out many comfortable years in Europe. It was during this time that he penned his magnum opus, *How to Trade in Stocks*.

In this book, Livermore laid out a number of rules that he believed, when followed to the tee, guaranteed day trading success (in fact, he attributed every one of his bankruptcies to breaking his own trading rules). In summation, these rules broadly state that traders should avoid trading every day of the year (reserving their trades for days on which the market is clearly experiencing either an upswing or downswing) and that traders should only enter a trade after the market has shown their speculation to be true (but that they should hasten to invest once this has happened).

Unfortunately, Livermore's tumultuous career and difficult upbringing eventually caught up with him and deepened the depression that he had already been suffering from. This led to him taking his own life in 1940 at the age of 63.

This is the inherent danger of day trading. You could lose everything, but that doesn't mean that there aren't ways to protect yourself. Logically, if you don't invest all of your money into day trading stocks, you can't lose all of it. If you're planning on embarking on day trading, it's a good idea to avoid investing more than 1% of your investment capital in any single trade.

Many online stock brokerage firms, like Interactive Brokers, TD Ameritrade, and Tradestation, offer day trading platforms to their account holders. This means that getting started is as easy as clicking through to one of their websites and setting up an account.

Position Trading Might Not Be in The Kama Sutra, But You Can Still Have A Good Time Doing It

If Jesse Livermore's tragic story nearly scared you off of the stock market entirely, you might be better suited to position trading. Position trading is far more passive than day trading is as it involves buying long term growth stocks. This means that a position trader might invest in a stock like Beyond Meats (which is an up and coming company with incredible potential for growth) for $80 in 2020, and hold onto it until 2030 (at which time the "green revolution" should have increased its value tenfold).

Position trading doesn't demand nearly as much of your time as day trading will. This is because once a position trader has executed a trade, it's bound to be months (if not years or decades) before he or she has to execute another. Consequently, this form of trading suits individuals who are not planning on leaving their full-time employment in order to invest in the stock market, or those who would simply like an investment to cash-in on in the future. Position trading can also save you a pretty penny on commissions and fees because stocks aren't constantly entering and exiting your portfolio (this, in turn, means your broker or brokerage firm doesn't have to process as many trades as it might have had to if you were engaged in day trading).

One of the downsides of position trading is that it only really works in a sustained bull market. Imagine how frustrated and disheartened you'd be if you bought a stock for position trading at $20 per share in 2020, only to have it be worth a mere $5 in 2030 (this means you would have waited a decade to make a 75% loss).

The most difficult part of position trading is spotting stocks that have the potential for immense growth over a longer period of time. Luckily modern technology has made it a lot easier for investors to do so. Some companies offer free online stock screening services. These 'stock screeners' allow you to choose the characteristics that you're looking for in a stock (for example, the likelihood of long term growth). TD Ameritrade, Zacks, Google Finance, and FinViz all offer free stock screeners on their websites that you can use to help you choose your next investment in the stock market.

You don't need a special kind of account in order to start trading by using this strategy, which means that any trading account will do.

Swing Trading: A Strategy That Surprisingly Has Nothing To Do With Bored Old Married Couples

Swing trading is something between day trading and position trading. It involves buying growth stocks with the intention of keeping them for a number of weeks or months and then reselling them, consequently profiting off of their growth over that time period. Swing traders don't hold on to their stocks for quite as long as position traders do, but they don't sell them quite as quickly as day traders do either.

Swing trading is a good option for stock traders who would like to make stock trading their full-time profession, but who don't want to be glued to a computer screen for most of the day like day traders often are. It provides investors a steady stream of income, however, it does require a certain level of competence in technical analysis as intermediate term stock price movements can be some of the hardest to predict. Although it can take the place of full-time employment in an investor's life, it's often actually statistically less profitable than position trading is because the stock price's upward movement is considerably less over an intermediate period of time than it is over a longer period of time.

You can simplify swing trading by investing in stocks whose stock charts show that their prices move up and down in predictable ways. For example, shares whose stock charts show that they experience a downswing or upswing in price every 50-days are a good swing trading investment. A number of ideal swing trading stocks have already been recognized by successful swing traders, these are Apple, Facebook, and Microsoft. Apple is a fantastic stock to teach beginner swing traders how to profit off of and track market-changing news. This is because Apple is constantly releasing new products, and its stock price predictably spikes after these products are announced, and then again when they're physically released. Traders who are willing to do a little bit of homework should find Apple stocks relatively easy to successfully swing trade by purchasing them during a bearish phase in the market and selling them shortly after the announcement or release of a new product. Facebook and Microsoft's stock charts also show regular troughs and peaks. This means that traders who are willing to go and map out trend lines onto these charts can easily predict when the stock's price is due to fall or climb again.

Of course, most stocks' price movements aren't nearly as clear-cut as Microsoft, Apple, and Facebook's are, which means that they're a lot more difficult to profitably swing trade. Luckily help is out there. Quite a number of successful swing traders voluntarily offer classes and seminars, and many even take on mentees. Mark Minervini offers mentoring, interactive online training, buying and selling tips, and archives that allow you to view his past trades through his web-based mentee program called Minervini Private Access. Dan Zanger, who has made millions and millions of dollars on the stock market, also mentors upcoming traders through his trading service called Chartpattern. Chartpattern's crowning glory is the daily newsletter penned by Zanger that it hosts. This newsletter contains charts, graphs, statistics, and a whole heap of trading tips telling you which stocks to buy and which stocks to sell. Alternatively, you can follow Trader Stewie (@traderstewie) on Twitter. He regularly posts stock charts, commentary on the aforementioned charts, and trading tips, and has amassed quite a following of dedicated fans (which means that he must be doing something right).

Scalping: Not As Brutal As You'd Think

Scalping might sound like a fate that might befall a character in an old Western movie, but it's actually a type of day trading. In fact, it's day trading taken to the extreme. Traders who make use of this strategy trade stocks by the second or minute, buying stocks in the hope of selling them for perhaps half a cent more each within a couple of moments. Scalpers don't wait for a stock's price to peak before selling it, they sell it the moment that it is worth more than they bought it for.

For example, someone making use of this strategy might buy 100,000 stocks for $3.01 and sell them for $3.02 two seconds later, making a profit of $100 within the blink of an eye. Of course, you would need to execute hundreds of trades every day in order to make a living off of scalping — which many traders do.

The pros and cons of day trading are amplified in relation to scalping. Scalping offers investors an even faster way to make a small fortune, but it costs one to get started too. You need a substantial amount of capital to buy 10,000 shares in order to make $100 off of a $0.01 price difference, especially when you consider that you'd need $40,000 in order to pull off this trade if the underlying stock costs $4 per share.

Scalpers make use of a number of techniques in order to determine which stocks are about to experience a short term spike in price, although they mainly rely on making use of an oscillator to determine whether a stock is overbought or oversold. An oscillator takes a stock's chart and replots it between two chosen points in order to indicate upward or downward trends. There are five types of oscillators that are commonly used: momentum, rate of change, moving average, relative strength index, and slow stochastic.

Momentum oscillators don't reflect a stock's actual price or the change of its price over time, instead it shows the upward or downward trajectory of the stock's price (and the rate of this increase or decrease) over time. A stock's momentum is calculated by subtracting its price at the beginning of the measured period from its current trading price.

Rate of change oscillators are similar to momentum oscillators in the sense that they depict the change in a stock's price over time instead of its actual trading prices. A stock's rate of change is calculated by taking its current price and dividing it by its price at the beginning of the observed period. A stock's rate of change is normally given in the form of a percentage or fraction.

Moving average oscillators plot out a stock's moving average over a period of time over that specific share's stock chart. They're used to measure a stock's divergences, to identify deviations between its moving averages, and to depict its moving average crossings. A moving average oscillator's "signal line" is a black line that represents the stock's entire moving average over the time period which the chart is plotted against. Scalpers know it's time to sell a particular stock when its moving average on a particular day moves above its signal line, and they know it's time to buy when its moving average on a particular day moves below its signal line.

A stock's relative strength is determined by comparing its growth to that of the average stock trading on the same stock exchange. Consequently, relative strength index oscillators show a stock's price movements over a period of time when compared to those of the rest of the stocks trading on the same stock exchange. A stock's relative strength index value is calculated by adding 0.01 to the stock's relative strength value, and then subtracting this total from 100. If a stock's relative strength index oscillator indicates that it has a relative strength index value of more than 75%, it's time to sell. If a stock's relative strength index oscillator indicates that it has a relative strength index value of less than 25%, it's time to buy.

Slow Stochastic oscillators are plotted using a stock's opening and closing prices over a predetermined period of time. Just as is the case with relative strength index oscillators, the value which they generate is measured in a percentage or fraction. Similarly, you should also sell a stock when its slow stochastic value is more than 75%, and buy when its value is less than 25%.

How To Get A Leg Up: Dollar-Cost Averaging and Algorithmic Trading

There are several trading strategies which investors can use to get a leg-up on their competition. One of these strategies is called dollar-cost averaging, and it's much simpler than it sounds. Ordinarily, you'd buy the batch of stocks you're interested in investing in in one transaction, amassing anything from a handful to hundreds of stocks belonging to the same company at once. If you are making use of dollar-cost averaging, you abstain from investing in all of the stocks you're interested in in one fell swoop, instead opting to invest a predetermined amount of money in the stocks that you are interested in at set intervals in time. The effect of this is that you end up buying fewer stocks belonging to a specific company when its stock price is high, and more when the stock price is low.

For example, a trader making use of this strategy might decide to invest $1,000 in Apple every month. During the first month, he or she might buy five shares in Apple for $200 per share, during the second month he or she might buy four shares in Apple for $250 per share, and finally, in the third month, he or she might buy eight shares for $120 per share. As a result of the trader staggering his or her investments in this way, he or she ends up paying an average price of $174.12 per share — whereas if he or she had invested the entire $3,000 at once during the first month, he or she would have paid an average price of $200 per share.

Dollar-cost averaging is a brilliant technique to employ in a bull market as it allows you to absorb some of the price hikes which are common in such an economic climate. This technique should, however, be reserved for long term stocks as the stock market's inherent volatility makes it an impractical short term investment strategy.

Another easy way to out-do the average trader's performance is by making use of algorithmic trading (which is also known as automated trading).

Algorithmic trading allows you to step away from the computer screen and get some fresh air, while still enabling you to execute trades as often as a scalper or day trader might. It involves using computer software in order to preprogram trading parameters. These trading parameters tell the program when to buy stocks, when to sell stocks, and for how much. As soon as these trading parameters are met, the program executes the trade — this means that you don't need to be ever-present or constantly alert of what's happening in your portfolio in order to profit off of the stock market. Not only is algorithmic trading less of a hassle than most traditional trading strategies are, algorithmic trading accounts are also usually much cheaper in respect of commissions, fees, and trading costs (this makes it the cheapest high-frequency trading option). The main advantage of algorithmic trading is that it removes the 'human factor' from the equation. Trading errors that might have been committed because of panic or over-excitement are eliminated completely because the underlying computer program is unaware of market sentiment and just continues trading within the parameters which you have set for it.

Unfortunately, you need a few things in order to get started with algorithmic trading. Firstly, you either need to be an experienced computer programmer yourself so that you can program your own trading algorithm, or you need to hire a programmer to do it for you. Luckily if you're willing to put your faith into someone else's programming capabilities, you could also make use of a pre-made, purchasable algorithmic trading program.

You also (obviously) need internet connectivity in order to run an algorithmic trading program on a live stock exchange.

There are a number of different algorithmic trading techniques. The most popular ones are trend-following, arbitrage, index fund rebalancing, and trading range.

Trend following is the most common algorithmic trading technique. Traders who make use of this technique try to follow trends in the stock market by setting their algorithmic trading software to execute trades based on a stock's technical indicators (like its price level movements, moving averages, and channel breakouts).

Arbitrage is one of the most profitable algorithmic trading techniques. It involves programming your algorithmic trading software to seek out trades where it's possible to buy a stock for a lower price on one stock exchange, and then to sell it for a higher price on another.

Index funds often sell off some of the shares held within their portfolios in order to maintain synergy with the stock index that they are trying to mimic — this is known as index fund balancing. Algorithmic traders often set their software to execute trades with index funds when they start selling off their stocks because index funds usually pawn off stocks that are no longer relevant to their portfolios at discounted prices.

Traders who swear by the trading range technique believe that stocks have an average price range which they rarely move out of. Consequently, they argue that determining a stock's average price range and using it to set algorithmic trading software's parameters is the most profitable way of algorithmic trading. This technique sees investors programming their algorithmic software to buy stocks when their price falls below their normal average price range, and to sell them when they rise above it.

Chapter 4:

You Don't Have To Do It

Alone

Doing anything alone is scary, that's why we take friends along when we're getting a new tattoo or going bungee jumping. Trading stocks might feel like a very lonely thing to do, especially when you consider that most of it takes place online, but it doesn't have to be. Including people on your journey to wealth is not only likely to make you a bit more daring, but it will keep your morale up too.

Having people to support you on your journey might even help you to make better stock trading decisions. Research conducted by Robert Dunbar, a psychology professor at Oxford University, found that people with more friends measured higher in intelligence quotient (IQ) tests than those with fewer friends. Having a close-knit group of amigos might also help you to become a more successful trader by increasing your social circle (and perhaps putting you into contact with other traders or brokers) as your friends' friends often become your friends.

The people that you choose to surround yourself with are just as important as the stocks that you choose to invest in.

Role Models Aren't Just For Children

You probably haven't consciously chosen a role model since you were a child, but that doesn't mean that you're not unconsciously mimicking those who you perceive to be successful. Studies have found that we take on the characteristics and traits of those we admire. This hammers an important point home: who we admire is important. Sometimes we idolize bad role models without even noticing it. We might think a character in a television series which we love is cool, or we might look up to a Twitter or Instagram personality — but these aren't necessarily people who we want to embody in our professional lives. For this reason, it's important to have business role models too.

Of course, the stock market can be a murky pond to try to find a role model in. A number of well-known traders may be financially successful but achieved that success at the cost of remaining ethical. There's no point in amassing millions if you're going to be remembered as the person who stepped on people's heads in order to climb the ladder to success, so there's no point in idolizing people who have gotten rich at the expense of others. Luckily there are still quite a number of ethical stock market role models to look up to, like Peter Thiel and Mark Cuban.

Peter Thiel was born in Frankfurt in Germany in 1967, but spent time living in South Africa and Namibia (then called South West Africa) as a child before his family settled down in the United States of America for good. He studied law through Stanford University, and ended up working for Sullivan and Cromwell in New York as a lawyer.

He soon grew weary of the legal profession and has previously stated that he felt that there had to be 'more' out there for him. This drove him to resign in favor of a position at Credit Suisse, an investment bank, as a derivatives trader. He stayed on at Credit Suisse until 1996, at which point he started wondering whether it wouldn't perhaps be better to own a publicly-traded company than it is to own stocks in publicly-traded companies.

In 1998 Thiel founded Confinity alongside Max Levchin. It was this company that went on to introduce PayPal to the general public in 1999. Thiel and his company then went on to sell PayPal to eBay in 2002. Thiel reinvested the profits he made from this sale in his new start-up company, Clarium Capital, a hedge fund that traded in equities, commodities, currencies, and interest rates.

Thiel is a self-confessed J.R.R. Tolkien fanatic, and this was reflected in the name of his next venture. Thiel founded Palantir (named after an artifact in the *Lord of the Ring* trilogy), a data analysis company, in May of 2003 and continues to serve as its chairman to this day.

You would think that after having a hand in the creation of three major enterprises, Thiel would slow down — but you'd be wrong. He went on to create Founders Fund (a venture capital fund), Valar Ventures (a venture firm), and Mithril Capital Management. Thiel also became a partner of Y Combinator in 2015, and purchased a 10% share in Facebook in 2004 as part of an angel investment.

Thiel has a net worth of $2.3 billion as of April of 2020. His business acumen is more than enough to warrant him 'role model' status, but it's not his only favorable characteristic. Thiel is quite a philanthropist too. He has donated, either personally or through his foundation, approximately $1.5 million to the Machine Intelligence Research Institute (an institute that is researching and trying to improve on artificial intelligence) over the years, as well as donating $7 million of his personal funds to Methuselah Mouse Prize (a company that is researching ways to slow or halt the aging process), and $1.75 million to the Seasteading Institute (a company which is working on developing underwater ocean communities).

Mark Cuban was born in 1958 in Pittsburgh, Pennsylvania to a middle-class Jewish family. His father upholstered the inside of cars, and his mother spent her life hopping from one profession to the next. Cuban started becoming interested in earning money at age 12 after he had started selling garbage bags in order to earn a bit of extra cash. This led to him spending his teenage years trying to make a quick buck. He did everything from selling stamps to running an extended paper route during the Pittsburgh-Post Gazette strike of the time. Cuban went on to study a Bachelor of Science in management through the Kelley School of Business.

In 1980 he founded his own company called MicroSolutions after being fired from his job as a salesman at Your Business Software. Ten years later Cuban sold MicroSolutions to CompuServe, and made approximately $2 million in profit from the deal. Five years later he started a company named Audionet (which facilitated the streaming of the first online Victoria's Secret fashion show) with Chris Jaeb. Audionet's name was changed to Broadcast.com in 1998 and a year later it was sold to Yahoo! for nearly $6 billion worth of stocks. Cuban went on to acquire Landmark Theatres in 2003, and is involved with 2929 Entertainment, AXS TV, Synergy Sports Technology, Ice Rocket, RedSwoosh, Brondell Inc, Sharesleuth.com, Bailoutsleuth.com, Magnolia Pictures, and the Dallas Mavericks.

Cuban currently has a net worth of about $4.3 billion and just like Thiel, he's a bit of a philanthropist. He created the Fallen Patriot Fund in 2003 in order to give aid to soldiers who had participated in the Iraqi war and their families. He has also helped Indiana University to upgrade their sport facilities through funding.

There's only one problem with this short list of stock market role models (who use their powers for good), it's lacking in female representatives. Unfortunately, the stock market has, perhaps not purposefully, been excluding women from trading for hundreds of years. Approximately 74% of American stock traders are men, this means that only 26% are women. Female role models can be hard to come by when they only make up a quarter of all traders and when their successes are less likely to be reported on by the media. In fact, a study conducted by Merrill Lynch found that nearly half of all female investors don't have a role model or someone who they aspire to be like. The stock market doesn't particularly market itself towards women either in the sense that it purposefully markets itself by portraying male ideals. For example, in 2018 E-Trade Financial launched a massive advertisement campaign that centered around a television ad showing a group of men being worshipped by a horde of scantily clad women while sipping on drinks on a yacht. It goes without saying that the "American Dream" that they're trying to sell is centered around a man's fantasy world, not a woman's.

While women might feel excluded, they should absolutely not be put off of investing. Women are better stock traders than men. It's true. A study conducted by Warwick Business School in 2018 found that female traders outdid male traders by about 1.8

percentage points, and it's not the only study that suggests that women are better at trading. When analyzing their eight million clients' accounts, Fidelity Investments also found that accounts belonging to their female clients outperformed their male clients' portfolios by 0.4%. Research conducted by Hargreaves Lansdown found that a woman was expected to make 25% more profit off of trading than a man would over a thirty-year trading period. Analysts theorize that the reasons why women are better traders are that they're less likely to take risks or invest in risky stocks, they invest the majority of their capital in funds (and not in individual stocks like many men do), and they trade less frequently (studies have found that the average male intermediate term trader conducted 13 trades over a one year period, while the average female intermediate term trader only conducted nine over the same time period).

Luckily if you're willing to look a bit further than all of the mainstream "investor role model" lists, you will find a number of brilliant women investors that are worthy of admiration.

Geraldine Weiss was born in San Francisco in the late 1920s. Not much is known about her early childhood, although it is known that she graduated with a degree in Business and Finance from the University of California in 1945. After completing her studies Weiss struggled to find employment, only receiving offers for secretarial positions and being denied the opportunity to interview for investors' vacancies despite the fact that she was more than qualified to fill such a position. Weiss became incredibly frustrated with her lot and decided to start publicizing her own investment column, titled *Investment Quality Trends*, at the age of 40 in the hope of proving her capabilities as a trader and investment advisor.

She initially made the mistake of penning her column under her own name, but after receiving a barrage of letters from men explaining in colorful detail what they'd rather do first before taking investment advice from a woman, she opted to sign it as the gender-neutral "G. Weiss." The popularity of her investment advice skyrocketed immediately and she soon came to be known as "the Dividend Detective." She finally revealed that she was a woman in the 1970s, by which time her investment advice had become law. Her investment column is still being published to this day, and she still has a hand in its production at the incredible age of 94.

Many influential modern stock traders attribute their success to following Weiss's stock screening rules. Weiss believed one should only invest in a stock if its dividend yield is undervalued, if the stock's holding company has managed to pay out compounded dividends of at least 10% to its investors over the past 12 years, if its book value is two or lower, if it has a price to earnings ratio of less than 20:1, if its dividend payout ratio is less than 50%, if the stock's holding company's debt is less than half of its total market capitalization, and if it classifies as a 'blue chip' stock.

Geraldine Weiss is only one of many remarkable women involved in the stock market. Muriel Siebert (or 'Mickie' to her friends) was born in 1928 in Cleveland in Ohio, and she was the first woman to ever own a seat on the New York Stock Exchange. After completing high school, she enrolled in Case Western Reserve University, however, she never completed the degree which she had been studying towards as her father fell ill shortly after she had started her studies, delving her personal life into chaos.

The fact that she hadn't actually completed a degree in business, finance, or economics, didn't hold her back. Siebert was noticeably bright, and this marked intelligence soon saw her being offered internships at a number of prominent financial institutions. By 1967 Siebert was sure she knew all she needed to know, and chose to shun employment at an established brokerage in favor of opening her own company, Muriel Siebert & Co. Inc. Initially, this company didn't do much other than selling technical analysis reports and performing risk assessments for larger investment or brokerage firms, but within a couple of months, Siebert was able to apply for a seat on the NYSE.

As was customary at the time, Siebert required sponsorship from someone who was already a part of this stock exchange in order to be afforded a seat. This means that she had to get a man to vouch for her capabilities, a tall ask in the 1960s. The first nine out of ten men which Siebert approached jovially brushed off her desperate plea for sponsorship. Once she managed to secure a sponsor, the bigheads at the NYSE decided to roll yet another boulder onto her path to success. They requested that she provide a guarantee from the bank stating that they would issue her a loan to cover $300,000 of the seat's total price of $445,000. This request had never been made to anyone looking to buy a seat on the NYSE previously, and was a clear attempt to sabotage Siebert's attempts at listing her company. After jumping through numerous hoops to prove her worth, Siebert was finally able to get the seat that she had been vying for in December of the same year. Her financial success didn't end there though. In 1977 she was made Superintendent of Banks in New York by the governor at the time, Hugh Carey. Her company, Muriel Siebert & Co. Inc., also merged with a furniture company called J. Michael & Sons in the 1990s. This saw Siebert's company being traded publicly for the first time.

Siebert spent her life not only proving her financial position, but trying to improve the world around her. In 1998 she was elected as the president of the New York Women's Agenda (NYWA). She used the power that came with this position to kick start a financial literacy program for women which was (and still is) offered through the NYWA. She also started a program called Siebert Entrepreneurial Philanthropic Plan in Muriel Siebert & Co. Inc. This program donates 50% of all of the profits it makes from new securities to a charity of the person who issued the security's choice.

Siebert passed away in 2013, but her legacy lives on through her philanthropy and her legacy as a warrior for women's rights.

There's no lack of positive role models in the stock trading world if you're willing to sieve through a few traders to find those who are truly inspirational and who uphold the same kind of values and moral ideals that you do.

Why Support Networks Are More Important Than Financial Networks

While it would definitely be an advantage if you could manage to befriend one or two world-renowned stock traders, they're actually not the connections that are the most vital to your success on the stock market. Your friends and family are. I know that sounds incredibly soppy (especially when stock traders are usually portrayed as cold-blooded and distant), but it's true. Science has proven it again and again.

A psychology professor named Dennis Proffitt conducted a study in 2008 in which he placed groups of students at the bottom of a series of hills and asked them to rate their steepness on a scale of one to 10. He found that students who were grouped with their friends rated the hills as being less steep than students who had been grouped with strangers. He hypothesized that this proved that people viewed challenges as less difficult to complete when they're surrounded by people that they're comfortable with. Making a million on the stock market might seem like Mount Everest to you right now, but you could scale it down to the size of a large hill if you have a solid support network around you.

Having a few good buddies can also buy you some extra time to trade stocks. In fact, it can buy you some extra time here on Earth. A study titled *Effect of Social Networks on 10 Year Survival in Very Old Australians*, which was conducted by Lynne Giles and a team of researchers in 2005, found that people who described themselves as having many friends were approximately 20% less likely to die a premature death than those who described themselves as having few friends. It's not the only study to draw this correlation either. Research that was published in the Journal of Oncology in 2006 suggests that having a close-knit group of friends is likely to help you survive serious bouts of illness. The study drew this conclusion after observing a group of 3,000 nurses who had been diagnosed with breast cancer and finding that those who had many close friends were four times less likely to die from their diagnosis when compared to their lonelier peers. A study printed in the journal called Proceedings of the National Academy of Sciences in 2015 also found that loneliness increases one's risk of developing hypertension by 124% (hypertension, in turn, increases one's risk of developing diabetes).

Not only will having a support network buy you a few extra years in which to trade stocks and spend time with your loved ones, but it can also make you smarter. A study titled *Psychosocial Working Conditions and Cognitive Complaints among Swedish Employees* which was published in 2013 found that workers who regularly spent time with friends were less likely than those who spent less time around friends to experience insomnia, concentration- or memory problems over the course of their lifetimes. Research published in the Journal of Neurology Neurosurgery and Psychiatry in 2012 also found that people who reported feeling less lonely were less likely to develop dementia by about 8%. It goes without saying that an improved memory and concentration span can go a long way in helping you to maximize your profits on the stock market.

Not every single one of your family members is guaranteed to fall in love with the idea of you investing in the stock market, in fact, there's bound to be a few naysayers in your midst. Luckily all of your family members don't need to be on board in order for you to reap the rewards of a social network. Research published by William Chopik in the scientific journal titled Personal Relationships found that friends were more important to one's overall well being than family was.

The Benefits of Having a Financial Advisor or Investment Coach

Financial advisors are professionals with Series 65 licenses that are registered as Registered Investment Advisors (RIAs) through the Securities Exchange Commission (SEC) who work either individually or through a firm in order to provide financial, investment, insurance, and estate advice to clients for compensation. A number of different kinds of professionals, namely insurance or stockbrokers, financial planners, tax preparers, estate or investment managers, and bankers, can be classified as financial advisors. The main characteristic that separates financial advisors from your average stockbroker or banker is that they offer advice on which moves they think their client should make next. They may even act on behalf of the client, closing deals and making investments with the client's capital without his or her express consent for every transaction.

Financial advisors all have different fee structures, some are fee-only, while others are commission only or fee-based with commission compensation. Fee-only financial advisors either charge their clients a percentage of the value of the stock's held in their portfolio or a set annual retainer fee. Commission only financial advisors, as the name suggests, operate on commission (a percentage of every trade's value) alone — this is probably the rarest fee structure among financial advisors. Fee-based with commission compensation financial advisors usually charge a lower annual retainer than fee-only financial advisors do, but they make up for it by charging a commission fee on every transaction (although this fee is usually less than the commission fee charged by commission only financial advisors).

If you're looking to employ a financial advisor, you don't have to look any further than The Garrett Planning Network or The National Association of Personal Financial Advisors, both of which list accredited financial advisors located right across the United States of America.

Investment coaches aren't quite as hands-on as financial advisors are. Their main duty is to help you to increase your financial status through education, motivation, and personalized lifestyle and investment advice. They don't actively control your portfolio, nor do they usually have access to it. This means that you get to choose whether to follow their advice, and which bits of their advice to follow. Investment coaches aren't regulated by legislation like financial advisors are, this means that you have to put a lot more research into picking a reputable one. You should choose an investment coach based on whether he or she has been financially successful themselves and on whether this financial success was gained through fees charged for coaching or money made through actual investment strategies (naturally the latter is preferable). Reputable investment coaches should also have contactable references, whom you should definitely contact in order to make sure that his or her other clients are happy with his or her services.

Twenty years ago you might have had to go see your investment coach at his or her offices at least once a week, but currently, most investment coaches offer their services remotely. This means that you can expect a phone call every week from your investment coach, as well as follow-up emails in between. This is convenient for traders who do not have the time to regularly meet their mentors during the week. Investment coaches generally charge their clients a monthly fee, that usually ranges from $1,000 per month to $2,000 per month, unlike financial advisors who charge annual retainers or who are paid a commission fee for every trade they conduct (this normally makes investment coaches the more economical option).

Financial advisors and investment coaches can both help you to become the millionaire you dream of being, but they serve different purposes. An investment coach is there to help you to raise capital in order to make investments by tweaking your lifestyle and spending habits, while a financial advisor helps you to manage your investments (and may even invest on your behalf).

Chapter 5:

Practice the

Unconventional

A large number of conspiracy theorists believe that the stock market is controlled by the Illuminati in furtherance of their "New World Order agenda." Unfortunately, the truth isn't nearly as exciting, but that doesn't mean that there isn't an element of magic and wonder to successful stock trading.

Businessmen will hardly, if ever, admit that they dabble in astrology or practice meditation — but don't let them fool you. A few prominent investors have been caught stating that they believe their success emanates from these practices, which means there must be something to it.

Forty-five percent of American adults believe in ghosts, and a great number believe that the Earth is flat, can it really be that hard to believe that these esoteric practices might hold some benefit?

The Answer is In Our Stars

John Pierpont Morgan Sr. (also known as J.P. Morgan), a successful stockbroker who dominated Wall Street in the late 1800s, once said; "Anyone can become a millionaire, but to become a billionaire you need an astrologer."

While I'm certain most of us would be content with millionaire-status, there's no reason why we can't make use of some of the billionaires' *'juju'* in order to help us make more money faster.

Most of us are only familiar with astrology as we've come to know it in newspapers or glossy magazines — as ambiguous four or five sentence snippets under each Zodiac that don't say very much of anything at all, but these hardly give one a proper idea of astrology's potential uses.

Human beings have been tracking the sun, moon, and stars' movements for thousands of years, in fact, scientists believe that they have found carvings in rock faces that depict celestial movements that might be up to 25,000 years old. However, the first definite case of the use of astrology in a manner that was similar to modern usage was documented in Mesopotamia in 1950 BCE (3,950 years ago). The Hellenistic Greeks were quick on their heels, and it wasn't long before astrology was as popular as wine in Greece. Of course, even back then it had its critics. Cicero, an ancient

Greek lawyer and philosopher, argued that there could be no merit to astrology because it based its prediction on birth charts (drawn up to depict the exact day, month, and year, on which a person was born). Cicero argued that even if two men were born on the same minute of the same day of the same month and of the same year, they would still likely be two very different individuals due to their upbringing, lineage, and health's effect on their lives' trajectories.

These two civilizations' astrology shared many common traits despite being about 1,600 years removed from each other. For example, they both believed in a norming point in Aries, planetary exaltations, the trine aspect, and dodecatemoria.

Egypt also had its own form of astrology, named the Dendera zodiac, that has been the cause of a few scientific rows. This is because researchers haven't been able to unanimously date it. Some, like Joseph Fourier, believe that it dates back all the way to 2,500 BCE (which would make it older than Mesopotamian astrology), while others, like Georges Cuvier, believe it originated in about 120 BCE. Strangely, despite the civilizations having only been properly introduced to each other in 332 BCE when Alexander the Great conquered Egypt, they share two common zodiac signs - the Scorpion and the Balance.

Medieval Europe saw a resurgence in astrology and zodiac reading, long after the astrologers of the ancient world had been forgotten. The first book, called *Liber*

Planetis et Mundi Climatibus, which discussed planetary movements' effects on the fates of men, was published by Gerbert of Aurillac in approximately 1020 AD. Thomas Aquinas, a prominent Dominican theologian during his time, also believed in the power of the stars to control men's everyday lives. He was able to reconcile this with his extreme faith in the Abrahamic God by believing, as stated in his writings, that the stars controlled men's destinies, but that God controlled their souls.

The practice of astrology became even more prevalent in Europe during the renaissance which began in the 1300s and lasted until the mid-1600s. In fact, it was so popular that nobility started hedging their bets on it. Both King Edward VI of England and Queen Elizabeth I of England had personal astrologers. King Edward VI of England's astrologer was an Italian polymath named Gerolamo Cardano. Cardano wasn't a stupid man or a gullible fool by any measure. This is made obvious by the fact that he was one of the mathematicians who pioneered the study of probability and introduced binomial theorem and binomial coefficients to the Western World. Queen Elizabeth I of England's astrologer was named John Dee. Dee coined the term "British Empire" in one of the predictions which he made to the queen, and was a respected mathematician and navigator (he trained many of the seamen who would set out on Britain's discovery voyages). Britain wasn't the only monarchy to take advice from the stars during the renaissance though: Tycho Brahe (who was also an alchemist) served as the Danish royal family's astrologer and Johannes Kepler (whose mathematical theories served as the starting point for Newton's laws of gravity) served as the Habsburgs' astrologer.

There are three branches of modern astrology: Western, Hindu, and Asian. Western astrology makes use of birth charts (as described above) to identify a person's tropical zodiac in relation to their equinoctial points. There twelve zodiacs also have twelve corresponding houses. These houses and zodiacs are based on the stars' and planets' placement at the time of a person's birth. Each one of the seven planets also represents one of the twelve zodiacs and one of the twelve houses.

Western astrology can be used both to make predictions about a person's future and to make predictions about a person's personality (and correlating personality weaknesses and strengths). While predictions about the future can be tricky, predictions about personality based on a person's zodiac sign are pretty unanimous.

Stock traders who aren't afraid of the supernatural can make use of these personality predictions in order to identify their shortcomings as traders.

The first sign of the Western zodiac is Aquarius, and it belongs to those born between January 20 and February 18. Aquarius' ruling planet is Uranus and it belongs to the eleventh house that represents friendship. Astrologers agree that Aquarius men and women are creative, visionary business-people with a soft spot for philanthropy and charity. Aquarians are also known to be quite frugal. The advice which Aquarians can take from this is to be careful not to give away too much of their capital to 'good causes' and not to invest in stocks simply because you agree with their environmental or humanitarian policies. Aquarians' creativity also makes them ideal high frequency traders, this means that you should theoretically look into either day trading or scalping if you're born under this sign.

The second sign of the Western Zodiac is Pisces. People who are born between February 19 and March 20 fall under this sign. Pisces is ruled by Neptune and belongs to the twelfth house which is known as the House of Spiritual Liberation. Pisces are natural-born empaths and artists. Pisces, just like Aquarians, tend to be a bit over-charitable with their money, and unlike Aquarians their zodiac dooms them to being terrible savers. Pisces dreamy nature may also make high frequency trading too exhausting for them, this means that they might be wise to stick with passive trading and investing in value stocks. With a little introspection, this personality prediction might help Pisces to realize that they need to be a bit more careful with their money (they might even be wise to enlist the services of an investment coach).

The third Western Zodiac is Aries — the bull-headed one represented by a ram's head (yes, they're a stubborn bunch). People who were born between March 21 and April 19 belong to this sign. Aries is ruled by Mars and belongs to the first house known as the House of the

Ascendant Mask. Aries is an active (often competitive) sign that needs to be wary of impulsivity. Aries are also brave and dynamic, as well as being excellent multi-taskers. Aries are natural-born leaders, which means that they usually stand-out well above the rest in the business world. The amalgamation of these traits can also make them fantastic stock traders. Aries's natural impulsivity is one of the few obstacles which they'll face as traders, but it can be easily overcome by setting limit orders on all of the trades which they're planning to conduct. Aries should also be careful of impulse buying stocks or other commodities without thoroughly researching them first.

The fourth sign of the Western zodiac is Taurus — the soft-hearted one represented by a bull's head. People born between April 20 and May 20 belong to this sign. Taurus is ruled by Venus and belongs to the second house known as the House of Resources (because Tauruses are so resourceful). Tauruses have small hearts and are easily hurt, even in business, which means that they tend to shy away from high risk stocks that could lead to either incredible returns or a humiliating failure (the risk of humiliation is often too daunting for them to even consider taking such a chance). Tauruses are also infamous hedonists, living for pleasure above all else and often ignoring the long term. Tauruses should be careful not to load their portfolios with short term stocks as these are often riskier (which could lead to the dreaded aforementioned humiliation) and ignore the importance of creating a solid financial future for yourself in favor of accruing wealth immediately.

The fifth sign of the Western zodiac is Gemini. People who are born between May 21 and June 20 belong to this sign. Gemini is ruled by Mercury and belongs to the third house known as the House of Open Perception. Geminis tend to be anxious individuals who are prone to indecisiveness, but on the flip side, they're quick learners with an inborn sense of curiosity. Geminis are also known for their quick wit and incredible intelligence, which must be why Jim Walton (the eighth richest man in the world) is born under this sign. Geminis' natural nervousness makes them hesitant investors, this in turn, increases their risk of missing out on profitable trades. For this reason, Geminis should strongly consider employing a financial advisor to handle their short term portfolios on their behalf, using their extraordinary intelligence to plan their long term portfolios personally.

The sixth sign of the Western zodiac is Cancer. People who are born between June 21 and July 22 belong to this zodiac. Cancer is ruled by the moon and belongs to the fourth house known as the House of Nadir (which represents home or the feeling of being at home). People who belong to this sign tend to be shy, intuitive, and overly emotional. Cancers are fantastic with money but they do not enjoy the stress of high risk investments. Cancers can make use of their extraordinary sixth sense to pick out stocks or funds to invest in, but should steer away from scalping or day trading which might prove too stressful.

The seventh sign of the Western zodiac is Leo. People who are born between July 23 and August 22. Leo is ruled by the Sun and belongs to the fifth house called the House of Joy and Bliss. Leo's are typically the life of the party. They're loud, colorful characters with a knack for charming onlookers. Leos won't find making friends in high places difficult as they manage to befriend just about anybody who crosses their path. Leos' ambitious and determined nature makes them ideal stock traders, however, they might struggle to find the time to get involved in high frequency trading due to their booming social lives. Leos should consider algorithmic trading to sponsor the flashy lifestyle that they likely desire as this will allow them to keep their free time (and time for drinks with friends).

The eighth sign of the Western zodiac is Virgo. People who are born between August 23 and September 22 belong to this sign. Virgo is ruled by Mercury and belongs to the sixth house, the House of Legacy, Lineage and Service. Virgos tend to be workaholics (and should be careful not to overwork themselves as this can lead to an emotional burnout) with incredibly keen, analytical minds. Their ability to keenly and accurately observe the world around them may cause them to be prone to anxiety disorders. Virgos's keen eye for detail makes them the ideal intermediate term growth stock traders, and their organizational skills mean that they're likely to be successful even without the guidance of a financial advisor or investment coach.

The ninth sign of the Western zodiac is Libra. People who are born between September 23 and October 22 belong to this sign. Libra is ruled by Venus and belongs to the seventh house, the House of the Descendant. Libras are fair-minded and diplomatic, but may be prone to bouts of depression and self doubt. Libras prefer having a lot of free (or rather, 'me') time, this means that they should steer clear of high frequency trading. People belonging to this sign should consider investing in funds that offer regular dividend payments in order to free up their time and to shield their investment choices from their own self doubt (which can lead to over-selling or hesitating to buy when the market is ripe).

The tenth sign of the Western zodiac is Scorpio. People who are born between October 23 and November 21 belong to this sign. Scorpio is ruled by Pluto and belongs to the eighth house, The House of Karma and Kali. Scorpio is the fiercest of the zodiacs. Scorpios are known for being cold-blooded, ruthless businessmen and -women who will stop at nothing to achieve their goals. They are usually highly intelligent, which makes them fantastic problem solvers. Scorpios can almost certainly turn their hand to any form of trading (though they'd likely be happiest in the high profit environment of high frequency trading) but should be careful not to engage in any unscrupulous practices which might land them in trouble further down the line.

The eleventh sign of the Western zodiac is Sagittarius. People who are born between November 22 and

December 21 belong to this zodiac. Sagittarius is ruled by Jupiter and belongs to the ninth house known as the House of Paradigms. People who are born under this sign are natural philosophers with a love for freedom, this means that they're often the sign that's the least likely to invest in the stock market as they don't see the point of material gains when they could be off hiking through some mountain range instead. Sagittariuses should realize that investing in the stock market is a fantastic way to fund their freedom, although it is recommended that they invest through a financial or robo-advisor as their impatient nature often drives them to buy or sell too soon.

The twelfth sign of the Western zodiac is Capricorn. People who are born between December 22 and January 19 belong to this sign. Capricorn is ruled by Saturn and belongs to the tenth house known as the House of Midheaven or Destiny. Capricorns are notoriously disciplined and self-controlled, this makes them the least likely to suffer any major losses on the stock market. Capricorns can turn their hand to nearly any stock trading strategy, but they'd probably be happiest investing in long term value stocks as their serious nature is likely to damper the thrill of any short term successes if there aren't also some long term prospects. People who are born under this sign are usually capable of managing their own finances and portfolios, but should strive to maintain a healthy work-life balance as Capricorns' focused nature can cause them to become obsessive.

Hindu astrology came into existence around the same time as Hellenistic Greek astrology did. It's rarely studied in the Western world, but has numerous parallels with Western astrology. It also consists of twelve zodiacs, namely: Meṣa (the ram), Vṛṣabha (the bull), Mithuna (the twins), Karka (the crab), Siṃha (the lion), Kanyā (the virgin girl), Tulā (the balance), Vṛścika (the scorpion), Dhanuṣa (the bow and arrow), Makara (the sea monster), Kumbha (the water pourer), and Mīna (the fishes). Hindu astrology also consists of a few tenants which don't appear in Western astrology, like lunar mansions (called nakṣhatras) and 'aspects' which indicate planets' relationships with each other and the zodiac itself (called Dṛṣṭis).

Asian astrology attempts to predict fates by making use of three enclosures, 12 'ci', and 28 celestial mansions. Just as is the case with Hindu and Western astrology, Asian (specifically Chinese) astrology can also be broken into twelve zodiacs, each represented by an animal, namely: the rat, the dragon, the ox, the tiger, the rabbit, the goat, the horse, the snake, the dog, the rooster, the monkey, and the pig.

Numerous stock traders have been recorded as attributing at least a measure of their success in trading stocks to astrology, and none more so than Arch Crawford who has been lovingly dubbed "Wall Street's astrologer." Crawford's track record speaks for itself.

He's been outperforming almost every other stock trader year after year, and has amassed a horde of rich and famous clients due to his success. He is also one of the few stock traders who managed to escape from the 2007 recession relatively unscathed. He was able to escape suffering any major losses by trusting the stars which told him to sell off his stocks a year prior and to invest in gold. Crawford is open about astrology's role in his stock trading success, and has often shared astrology tips for stock market trading during interviews. One of Crawford's hottest tips is that the stock market is at its most volatile directly before or directly after an eclipse.

Regardless of whether you believe that the stars are revealing their secrets to Crawford or whether you think he's actually just undermining his own skills as an analyst is up to you, although it definitely doesn't hurt to check your horoscope before planning any major trades. Those who would like to center their trading strategy around the stars should consider delving a bit deeper into celestial prediction techniques.

What Billionaires Can Learn From Tibetan Monks

Meditation isn't just something for college kids with long hair and leather sandals, a number of successful stock traders have taken it up and quite a good deal of them swear by its ability to make you a better trader.

We've known about the health benefits of meditation for ages. It reduces stress which decreases one's risk of suffering from stress-induced mental health problems or physical ailments (like post traumatic stress disorder, irritable bowel syndrome, and fibromyalgia). A study which was conducted in 2014 and was published in the journal titled *JAMA Internal Medicine* found that those who regularly reported meditating saw drastically decreased levels of cortisol (the stress hormone) and experienced a reduction of inflammation (which, in itself, aids in the symptomatic relief of a number of conditions). Scientists wondered whether meditation's ability to relieve stress would translate into it being an efficient way to control anxiety disorders, and surprisingly the answer was yes. Research conducted by Ruth Baer and James Carmody found that regular meditation was an effective treatment for a number of anxiety-related mental health problems, like paranoid thoughts, phobias, obsessive-compulsive behaviors, panic attacks, and social anxiety.

Studies even suggest that meditation might help you to become a better, smarter person. A study published in 2015 titled Reconstructing and Deconstructing the Self: Cognitive Mechanisms in Meditation Practice found that the introspection that meditation facilitates allows one to identify one's own character flaws and to work on them. This means that if impatience or nervousness is ruining your stock trading career that you could change its trajectory by taking up meditation. Meditation might even help you to become more creative and improve your problem-solving skills — both of which are abilities that can help you to up your stock trading game.

Not only can meditation help you to chill out, become a better person, and improve your creativity, but it can also improve your attention span (a trait that is incredibly important for high frequency traders). Research that was published by Fadel Zeidan and Susan Johnson in the journal *Consciousness and Cognition* in 2010 found that even just four days of regular meditation markedly improved the participants' concentration spans and memory. Another study which was performed by the University of California's Neuro-Imaging Laboratory found that meditators had more gyrification in their brains than non-meditators. Gyrification are the creases in your brain, and scientists believe that they're the parts of our brains that are responsible for logical decision making and processing new information.

There are a number of different kinds of meditation. The most popular kinds amongst stock traders are yoga and mindfulness meditation. We're all relatively familiar with yoga (in fact your local gym probably offers yoga classes), but few of us realize that it's a form of meditation. The breathing exercises and mantras that go along with yoga helps its practitioners to enter a meditative state, this means that they get to reap all of the wonderful benefits mentioned above whilst also improving their strength and flexibility. Mindfulness meditation, unlike your typical cross-legged, humming stereotype, can be practiced anywhere at any time. It involves becoming consciously acutely aware of your surroundings and the sensations and feelings in your own body.

Learning to center yourself and calm your mind can greatly improve your trading, and you really only need to commit about ten or fifteen minutes a day to do it (probably less time than you spend checking your emails or scrolling through social media in the morning).

Without Art, the Earth is Just 'Eh'

You might be wondering what art and stock market investing have to do with each other, especially considering that Picasso wasn't into finances and that Warren Buffett doesn't paint, but art may actually help you to improve your trading skills (although I doubt stock trading will improve your art skills, unless you're planning on "painting the tape").

Art has been around for nearly as long as modern human beings have (in fact, the oldest cave paintings are about 40,000 years old), and there's a reason why we took it up as soon as we learned to craft tools — it's good for us.

Stock traders should consider taking up an artistic hobby because, just as is the case with yoga and meditation, it can help to boost your mood and improve your mental health. Traders are especially prone to emotional burnouts and mental breakdowns brought on by the inherent stress of trading, this makes it all the more important to take care of your mental health in order to ensure that you don't have to deal with any interruptions caused by your psychological health in your trading career.

A study which was published in 2007, titled *The Neurological Basis of Occupation*, found that all artistic activities, including activities like knitting or sewing, increases the level of dopamine, the happy hormone, in one's brain and decreases the amount of cortisol in one's body. This means that engaging in a creative activity can leave you feeling happier, less stressed, and it can improve your physical health too. Cortisol, the stress hormone, has been found to cause and contribute to a number of life-threatening conditions, namely: heart disease, diabetes, asthma, local or systemic infections, and cancer. Catching or developing any one of these five conditions can put a serious damper on your ability to become the Wolf of Wall Street (it's difficult to conduct business from your sick bed or the grave). Dopamine isn't just responsible for making you feel giddy either. Increased levels of dopamine in one's brain can help it to absorb and retain information, this means that it increases one's memory and one's capacity for learning (both traits will undoubtedly make you a better trader). Research published by Anne Bolwerk and Jessica Mack-Andrick in 2014 even found that regularly engaging in a creative activity could increase one's resistance to the effects of cortisol (this means that you could develop somewhat of an 'anti-stress' superpower, like a cool-calm-and-collected Clark Kent).

Painting, writing, drawing, playing music, knitting, sewing, molding, sculpting, or beading can help you to become smarter too. Previously it was believed that people who were more intelligent than the average person had larger brains, but now we know that smarter people don't have larger brains — but they do have more neural connections. Your brain's neurons are constantly making new arrangements and changing themselves as you age (this is known as neural plasticity). People whose brains are capable of changing or creating new neural connections more often have been proven to be more intelligent. A study which was printed in the journal Neuroscience and Biobehavioral Reviews in 2015 found that those who regularly practiced an artistic pursuit increased their brains' neural plasticity, this means that the participants of this study literally made themselves smarter by spending a few minutes a day journaling, doodling, or knitting a sweater.

Committing a bit of time each day to an artistic pursuit might not help you to learn how to put your leg behind your head like yoga might, but it's a surefire way to combat the stressful competitive environment of the stock market and to stay at the top of your game.

Chapter 6:

Stock Trading as a

Business

No-one has ever become a millionaire or billionaire by half-heartedly trading stocks. You need to invest yourself fully and actually go for it, without making excuses. If you have your investment capital saved up, I challenge you to contact a brokerage tomorrow morning and to start trading with your chosen strategy, If you're not financially ready to start investing in the stock market, I dare you to choose an investment coach and to start following his or her advice immediately so that you can save up the investment capital which you need to finance your stock market journey. If you start investing a year sooner than you planned, you'll be rolling in dough a year sooner too.

Of course, getting started is a lot more daunting than it seems, especially because you probably don't want to lose your initial investment. Luckily you can improve your chances of success by managing your brokerage account like a business owner.

Before running off and registering your business, you need to decide what 'type' of business you'd like to register it as. You could register it as a sole proprietorship, a partnership, a limited liability company, or a corporation.

Sole proprietorships are businesses that have only one owner (and no shareholders or partners). People are fond of making use of this business format because it is relatively inexpensive to register, it usually doesn't have to pay business or company tax, and its accounting is as simple as keeping its books up to date. This business format shifts all of the business's liabilities onto the owner's shoulders, but it also allows the owner to pocket all of its profits.

Partnerships are also a popular choice because they facilitate the company's ownership by a number of different parties (who could either be people or other companies). Just like sole proprietorships, partnerships are cheap to form, however, owners are likely to draw less profits from them than they would from sole proprietorships because partnerships split the business's profits (and liabilities) equally between its partners.

Limited liability companies (LLCs) can't be formed in all states, although most do allow their registration, this is because it is a relatively new business structure which isn't quite as well established as the two structures that were discussed above. LLCs are legal entities that are capable of having their own liabilities, this means that any liability (like a loan) which an LLC takes on can't be transferred to one of its members (except for in exceptional circumstances). It is important to read up on your state's LLC rules and regulations before deciding on registering your business as one because rule pertaining to LLCs' continuity vary from state to state (with some states requiring that a future date be set for the company's dissolution upon registration, and with others requiring its dissolution upon the death or bankruptcy of one of its members).

Corporations are the most heavily taxed of the four aforementioned business structure options. Corporations take the separation of liability from their shareholders (their owners) a step further than LLCs do — when a corporation is registered, an entirely new "legal person" is created with rights and responsibilities similar to those that a 'natural person' (a human being) might have. Some of the additional responsibilities which corporations have are that they're required to convene an annual meeting of their shareholders in order to vote on important matters and plan the year ahead, and they're required to pass any major decisions by their board of directors before making them.

Not only will running your stock trading account like a business help you to set goals and draw up plans in order to meet them, but it can also offer you a few tax breaks as well as making it easier for you to secure financing through an accredited financial institution.

You should start off by incorporating your new stock trading 'business.' On a state or local level, incorporating a business is usually as easy as paying for and reserving a name for it. Normally states will only recognize your enterprise as a legitimate business if you have employees who reside in that state, if some of your enterprise's profits are generated within the state, if you operate your business within the state, or if you regularly meet with clients who live in that state.

Different states have different registration requirements, this means that it's important to check what your state's regulations are. Additionally, most states require that business owners also register their enterprises with a business bureau, business agency, or with the Security of State's office before the state itself will accept the business's registration.

Formally registering your business also means that you can start claiming back tax deductions for any applicable expenses which you may incur. These expenses are outlined in more detail in section 162 of the Internal Revenue Code, but broadly include general and administrative expenses, automobile expenses, entertainment and travel, depreciation, and employee benefits. General and administrative expenses include the cost of supplies and equipment, office rent, utilities, salaries, and accounting or legal fees. Your mileage or fuel costs for business-related travel classifies as an automobile expense (although you can't claim for the trips you have made to and from the office, only for trips to customers, seminars, or suppliers). The IRS usually only refunds about 50% of proven entertainment and expense amounts to its customers, however, this deduction can be claimed for anything from meeting with a client over a meal and some wine in a nice restaurant, to taking suppliers out for a golf day — these expenses are difficult to prove, so keep your receipt (and your excuse for why it was a necessary business expense) handy. Any equipment which you buy for your business depreciates the moment that you purchase it, luckily you can claim back an annual percentage of your equipment's value as depreciation too. Employee benefits can also be claimed back from the IRS, this includes any contributions which you may have made to employee's pension or annuity funds.

Once you've registered your business, you might want to look into acquiring a Series 7 license as well. This is a license that allows you to operate as a stockbroker, this means that you could add an extra branch of income to your stock market activities by being paid to trade on behalf of others as well. In order to acquire such a license, you need to sit a three hour and 45 minute long exam consisting of 125 multiple choice questions. It costs approximately $245 to sit the exam. You need to get a grade of at least 72% in order to pass the test, but passing is the easy part. In order to even be allowed to register to write the exam, you need to prove that you have sponsorship from a FINRA-registered company in order to write.

Running your stock trading enterprise as a business can exponentially increase your profits, and it's something that's completely achievable for your average Joe.

Conclusion

Having refreshed your memory on some stock market basics, you should feel ready and empowered to choose a stock trading strategy that will fit your desired lifestyle and financial goals like a glove. Furthermore, having identified positive stock trading role models, developed a strong support network, and perhaps even employed a financial advisor or investment coach, you should be well on your way to make millions. Billions? Well, that's achievable too (with some help from the stars or perhaps even a yogi master).

You might be thinking that becoming a millionaire is just a pipe dream, but hundreds of thousands of people before you have managed to achieve it, and hundreds of thousands of people after you will achieve it too. There's nothing stopping you from joining their ranks. At some point in his life, Warren Buffett didn't know that he was going to be a billionaire either. You now have all of the knowledge and tools you need to realize your financial dreams. A couple of months from now you could be looking to buy a private jet, or you could pay off your mortgage, your future is in your hands. Take the plunge, close your eyes, cross your fingers, and start trading like a millionaire today. There's no more time for excuses. Every day you delay is a day of wealth that you rob yourself of. You don't have to start by investing $10,000 (or $100,000), but you have to start. Even if it's with a couple of months' worth of savings. None of my advice will help you if you don't take a leap of faith.

Why don't you set yourself a financial goal in a review of this book, and check back in a couple of months' time to see if you've met it? I bet you'll be surprised to find that you'll not only be able to meet your financial goals, but to exceed them as well. A couple of years from now, you might be sipping fruity cocktails on your own personal yacht in the Bahamas, and you'll look back on that review and smile. Knowing where your journey started and how far you've come.

References

A Detailed Look at the Pisces Personality Profile and Description. (2010, March 24). Retrieved April 20, 2020, from https://astrologybay.com/pisces-personality-profile-description

AbhishekHi, K. (2018, May 27). Why do stock prices fluctuate? Retrieved April 12, 2020, from https://tradebrains.in/why-do-stock-prices-fluctuate/

Aquarius Zodiac Sign Aquarius Horoscope. (n.d.). Retrieved April 15, 2020, from https://www.astrology-zodiac-signs.com/zodiac-signs/aquarius/

Basu, C. (2017, February 7). Purpose of the Stock Market. Retrieved March 24, 2020, from https://finance.zacks.com/purpose-stock-market-2365.html

Beattie, A. (2020, April 5). The Birth of Stock Exchanges. Retrieved April 12, 2020, from https://www.investopedia.com/articles/07/stock-exchange-history.asp

Belfort, J. (2016). The Wolf of Wall Street Collection: the Wolf of Wall Street & Catching the Wolf of Wall Street. London: Two Roads.

Benefits of art therapy. (2012). Primary Health Care, 22(8), 13–13. doi: 10.7748/phc.22.8.13.s11

Braucher, D. (2019, November 6). How to Deal with Envy and Jealousy. Retrieved April 12, 2020, from https://www.psychologytoday.com/za/blog/lif e-smarts/201911/how-deal-envy-and-jealousy

Buffett, W., & Andrews, D. (2019). Warren Buffett: in his own words. Chicago: B2 Books, an Agate imprint.

Carter, Gary W. Small Business Tax Secrets: Ultimate Tax Savings for the Self-Employed!. John Wiley & Sons, March 2003

Cash, L. Stephen, and Thomas L. Dickens. New Home Office Rule Applies for 2000 Filing Season. Strategic Finance. February 2000.

Cheung, F. (2007). Mental training: The benefits of short-term meditation. Nature China. doi: 10.1038/nchina.2007.226

Cussen, M. P., Owyoung, P., Bank, E., & Nicholson, J. (n.d.). How to Start a Day Trading Business. Retrieved March 10, 2020, from https://www.sapling.com/4999847/start-day-trading-business.

Dailey, Frederick W. Tax Savvy for Small Business. Ninth Edition. Nolo Press, 2005.

Financial Advisor Or Investing Coach: Which Is Right For You? (n.d.). Retrieved March 10, 2020, from https://www.lifetimeinvestor.com/articles/financial-advisor-or-investing-coach/

Glossary of Stock Market Terms & Definitions. (n.d.). Retrieved March 29, 2020, from https://www.nasdaq.com/glossary

Haden, J. (2019, April 16). How Science Says People Who Get Rich Are Different From Everyone Else. Retrieved April 12, 2020, from https://www.inc.com/jeff-haden/how-science-says-people-who-get-rich-are-different-from-everyone-else.html

Hall, M. (2018, April 30). Understand the Basics of Astrology. Retrieved March 10, 2020, from https://www.liveabout.com/what-is-astrology-206723

History of the Stock Market. (2019, December 23). Retrieved April 11, 2020, from https://stock-market.laws.com/stock-market-history

How to Research Stocks: 4 Steps for Beginners. Retrieved March 10, 2020, from https://www.nerdwallet.com/blog/investing/how-to-research-stocks/

iFate. (n.d.). All About Capricorn. Retrieved April 20, 2020, from https://www.ifate.com/about-capricorn.html

Investing in Stocks with Basic Knowledge of Economics. (n.d.). Retrieved March 10, 2020, from https://www.dummies.com/personal-finance/investing/investing-in-stocks-with-basic-knowledge-of-economics/

Kalamakis, L. (2018, February 19). Should You Hire a Business Coach? Retrieved March 10, 2020, from https://freelancetofreedomproject.com/should-you-hire-a-business-coach/

Lakhiani, V. (2020, February 4). The 7 Types Of Meditation And Why They Should Be A Daily Practice For Everyone. Retrieved March 10, 2020, from https://blog.mindvalley.com/types-of-meditation/

List of Stock Exchanges – Major Stock Exchanges. (n.d.). Retrieved April 5, 2020, from http://www.trade.education/list-of-stock-exchanges/

McFarlane, G. (2020, January 29). The Differences Between Private and Public Equity. Retrieved April 12, 2020, from https://www.investopedia.com/articles/investing/030415/difference-between-private-and-public-equity.asp

Navin, J. (2018, July 14). Interview With Legendary Technical Analyst Arch Crawford: Astrology And The Stock Market. Retrieved March 10, 2020, from https://www.forbes.com/sites/johnnavin/2018/07/14/interview-with-legendary-technical-analyst-arch-crawford-astrology-and-the-stock-market/#258ddb601343

Poitras, G. (n.d.). From the Renaissance Exchanges to Cyberspace: A History of Stock Market Globalization. Handbook of Research on Stock Market Globalization. doi: 10.4337/9780857938183.00012Roebuck, E. (2018, April 26).

Sagittarius Zodiac Sign Sagittarius Horoscope. (n.d.). Retrieved April 20, 2020, from https://www.astrology-zodiac-signs.com/zodiac-signs/sagittarius/

Scorpio Zodiac Sign Scorpio Horoscope. (n.d.). Retrieved April 20, 2020, from https://www.astrology-zodiac-signs.com/zodiac-signs/scorpio/

Smith, A. (2016, October 26). How to Start a Stock Trading Business and Claim Tax Deductions. Retrieved March 10, 2020, from https://smallbusiness.chron.com/start-stock-trading-business-claim-tax-deductions-12333.html

Sykes, T. (2020, April 10). 37 Stock Trading Terms Every Trader Needs to Know. Retrieved March 10, 2020, from https://www.timothysykes.com/blog/trading-terms-you-need-to-know/

Taurus Zodiac Sign Taurus Horoscope. (n.d.). Retrieved April 20, 2020, from https://www.astrology-zodiac-signs.com/zodiac-signs/taurus/

The Investopedia. (2020, March 16). Why Would a Company Buy Back Its Own Shares? Retrieved March 28, 2020, from https://www.investopedia.com/ask/answers/042015/why-would-company-buyback-its-own-shares.asp

The Pros and Cons of Algorithmic Trading. Retrieved March 10, 2020, from https://education.howthemarketworks.com/pros-cons-algorithmic-trading/Segal

Trading As A Business - My Step By Step Guide. (2019, October 23). Retrieved March 10, 2020, from https://www.tradeciety.com/trading-business-step-step-guide/

U.S. Department of Treasury. Internal Revenue Service. "Forms and Instruction." Available from http://www.irs.gov/formspubs/lists/0,id=978 17,00.html. Retrieved on 17 May 2006

What Are Stocks and How Do They Work? (n.d.). Retrieved April 12, 2020, from https://www.wallstreetsurvivor.com/starter-guides/what-are-stocks-how-they-work/

What Is An Investment Coach? (n.d.). Retrieved March 10, 2020, from http://www.sageinvestors.ca/what-is-an-investment-coach

What is Astrology. (n.d.). Retrieved March 10, 2020, from https://cafeastrology.com/whatisastrology.html

White, E. (2019, June 6). Gemini: Characteristics and Personality Traits of Gemini. Retrieved April 20, 2020, from https://www.zodiacsigns-horoscope.com/gemini/gemini-woman-personality-traits/

White, E. (2019, June 6). Libra Woman: Characteristics and Personality Traits of Libra Female. Retrieved April 20, 2020, from https://www.zodiacsigns-horoscope.com/libra/libra-woman-personality-traits/

White, S. (2011). Stock Market Investing: Lessons from History. Consumer Knowledge and Financial Decisions, 303–313. doi: 10.1007/978-1-4614-0475-0_19

Wójcik, D. (2011). The Map of the Global Stock Market Redrawn: Stock Market Centres and their Future. The Global Stock Market, 151–170. doi: 10.1093/acprof:oso/9780199592180.003.0008

Yochim D. (2019, November 19). Stock Trading: How to Begin, How to Survive. Retrieved March 10, 2020, from https://www.nerdwallet.com/blog/investing/stock-trading-how-to-begin/Yochim, D. (2020, March 10).

Yochim, D. (2019, November 19). Stock Trading: How to Begin, How to Survive. Retrieved March 10, 2020, from https://www.nerdwallet.com/blog/investing/stock-trading-how-to-begin/

Yoga Study Finds Mix of Health Benefits. (2009). PsycEXTRA Dataset. doi: 10.1037/e510542010-010

Zodiac Signs- Aries. (n.d.). Retrieved April 20, 2020, from https://zodiac-signs-astrology.com/zodiac-signs/aries.htm

Zucchi, K. (2020, March 6). 4 Common Active Trading Strategies. Retrieved March 10, 2020, from https://www.investopedia.com/articles/active-trading/11/four-types-of-active-traders.asp